VIVIAN WOODWARD

FOOTBALL'S GENTLEMAN

VIVIAN WOODWARD

FOOTBALL'S GENTLEMAN

NORMAN
JACOBS

TEMPUS

First published 2005

Tempus Publishing Limited
The Mill, Brimscombe Port,
Stroud, Gloucestershire, GL5 2QG
www.tempus-publishing.com

British Library Cataloguing in Publication Data.
A catalogue record for this book is available from the British Library.

ISBN 0 7524 3430 6

Typesetting and origination by Tempus Publishing Limited
Printed in Great Britain

CONTENTS

INTRODUCTION AND ACKNOWLEDGEMENTS

My interest in Vivian Woodward was first aroused almost twenty years ago when I met his niece, Nora Timmens, a long time Clacton resident and vice-president of the Clacton and District Local History Society, of which I was Chairman. She told me a few stories about her famous uncle Jack, mostly concerning how he played football and cricket with her when she was a small girl, and showed me a few cuttings about him from old and yellowing newspapers as well as some other bits and pieces including the telegram her other uncle, Alex, had sent on the occasion of Uncle Jack's debut for the England football team.

I have to confess I had never heard of Vivian Woodward, even though I had taken an interest in football since I was a small boy in the 1950s. At the time I decided I would look into this famous uncle of hers when I had a bit more time. However, with other calls on my time it got pushed to the back of my mind and it wasn't until a few years later that my interest was revived.

While I was researching for a book I was writing on Colchester I met a man called Wally Lawrence, then in his ninety-fifth year. I had been introduced to Wally because he had once played football for Colchester's Culver Street Ironworks team in the North Essex League. He told me about his career as a footballer then said to me that nothing in his life had compared to the time he actually played against the great Vivian Woodward. My ears pricked up at this and I remembered my conversation with Nora. 'What was that like?' I asked. He told me about an incident that had occurred in the match. He recalled that at one point in the game, he mistimed a tackle on the great man and fell heavily on top of him. Wally apologised. Woodward's reply was, 'That's all right son, you were going for the ball. Just let me get up.' It made me wonder what sort of reply Wally would have got from some of today's top footballers! It also revived my interest and I decided I really had to find out more about this man.

As I started to research his life I couldn't believe what I was reading. Here was not only one of the greatest footballers ever produced by this country but also the perfect gentleman. And yet, whenever I mentioned his name most people looked blankly and said, 'Who?' I thought it was about time his story was brought to the attention of a wider public and that he at last got the recognition he deserved. And now, thanks to James Howarth and Holly Bennion at Tempus Publishing, I am able to do just that.

As well as James and Holly there are a number of people I should like to thank for their help in preparing this book. In particular, Andy Porter, Tottenham Hotspur's unofficial historian, who has given me a tremendous amount of help on Woodward during his Tottenham days. Also Mike Geen and Robert Stein for their help with the Chelsea days, George Hardwick for the Clacton period, Stella Lyne for help with the family tree and census returns, Bill Travers and Doris Ko of the Spencer Cricket & Lawn Tennis Club and David Barber of the Football Association; also to the staff of the British Olympic Committee, the British Library Newspaper Library at Colindale, the Public Record Office at Kew, Clacton Public Library and Haringey Archive Service at Bruce Castle. I would also like to thank Neal Harrington of the *Clacton Gazette* for permission to reprint part of the obituary to Vivian Woodward which appeared in the 5 February 1954 edition of the *East Essex Gazette*, also Peter Raath for permission to reprint the photograph of the England Touring Team of 1910 which appeared in his book, *Soccer Through the Years*, Roy Brazier for permission to reprint photographs which appeared in his book *Tottenham Hotspur Football Club 1882-1952* (Tempus Publishing Ltd, 2000) and Phil Neill for permission to reprint the Vivian Woodward card from his England's 'Top Goalscorers' set.

Just a brief word of explanation, particularly for younger readers. Vivian Woodward was playing at a time when the standard team formation was goalkeeper; right-back, left-back; right half, centre half, left half; outside right, inside right, centre forward, inside left, outside left. That is of course, in modern parlance, a 2-3-5 formation. This had been standardised in the 1890s and remained pretty much in force in Great Britain until Alf Ramsey became England manager in the early 1960s. These are the positions that will be referred to throughout the book.

ONE

THE CLACTON YEARS
(1879-1901)

Vivian John Woodward was born on 3 June 1879 at 10 Crown Villas, Kennington, Surrey. This was within a stone's throw of the Oval Cricket Ground, venue of the first FA Cup final in 1872 and home to Surrey County Cricket Club – a propitious start for the man who was to take the football world by storm and be no mean cricketer in to the bargain. He was the seventh of eight children born to John and Anna Woodward. John was, by profession, an architect and surveyor, and a prominent member of Lambeth society, being the District Surveyor, Chairman of the Lambeth Vestry, a Justice of the Peace and a Freeman of the City of London.

After Vivian was born, John and Anna Woodward began to think about taking their ever-growing family to sample the delights of the seaside and chose the newly founded resort of Clacton-on-Sea as the perfect place for a holiday. The Clacton-on-Sea of 1880 was a very different place to the lively, brash seaside resort it was to become noted as in the twentieth century. It had been founded only ten years previously to cater specifically for the wealthy upper middle classes. As yet, the railway did not reach Clacton and the main access to the town was by the paddle steamers which plied up and down the Thames disgorging passengers on to Clacton Pier.

The Woodwards made the holiday trip to Clacton regularly, staying in a house called Inglefield Villa in Ellis Road. In 1885, the Woodwards took a lease on the house and made it their own. John continued his work in Lambeth and joined the family at weekends and for several weeks during the summer. As the children got older, Anna too stayed in London with her husband, leaving the care of the smaller children in the capable hands of the eldest daughter, Annie. Being an architect, John's long-term plan was to build his own house. By 1892 this dream had become a reality as, approximately twelve years after their first acquaintance with Clacton, the Woodwards moved into their own property, a villa in Pier Avenue, designed and built by the head of the household, which they named Silvercloud. At the time, the Woodward residence marked the outermost limit of the new town.

Living so close to the Oval, it was only natural that John should be a keen sportsman. He is known to have turned out for the Clacton-on-Sea cricket team in the 1880s and early '90s and later, in 1898/99, became president of the Clacton Town Football Club. Also, during the 1890s, he was an organiser of one of Clacton's main holiday events, the Annual Regatta, which consisted of land sports as well as water sports. (Incidentally, although there seems to be no record of Vivian ever taking part, his older brother, Alexander, once came second in the 100 yards three-legged race with George Mathams.)

Around 1890, with the family now firmly ensconced at Clacton, Mr Woodward looked for a school for his second eldest son, Alexander, and his third eldest son, Vivian – the eldest son, Walter, was already a boarder at a school in Carshalton, Surrey, near their Kennington home. His love of sport led him to look round for a suitable school which excelled not only academically, but also in the sporting field. Every week, the local Clacton newspaper, the *East Essex Advertiser & Clacton News*, carried an advert for a school situated in Clacton High Street called Ascham College. The advert read: 'Boys well trained, surrounded by healthy moral and physical influences, for the Public Schools, Professional and Commercial life. Outdoor games and recreation encouraged. Every boy is taught to swim. More than EIGHTY CERTIFICATES have been obtained in 7 years at the College of Preceptors, the Cambridge Local and Trinity College Examinations.'

This sounded the ideal school for Mr Woodward, as Ascham College had a good reputation locally for its sporting activities: the Principal, Mr A.S. Wilson, was himself one of the founders and vice-presidents of Clacton Town Football Club. In fact, when Clacton was founded in 1892, some of their first practice matches were held on the Ascham College playing fields. Keen as he was for his sons to be able to take part in sporting activities, John sought an assurance from Mr Wilson that their academic careers would not suffer if they did so. Mr Wilson gave him the assurance he required and John agreed to send Alexander and Vivian to this fine educational establishment.

Soon both Alex and Vivian began to show promise in the sporting field, initially on the cricket pitch rather than the football field. Vivian first caught the eye when, at the age of only twelve, he was chosen for the Ascham College First XI and, by all accounts, eclipsed players four or five years older than himself. His first mention in the local paper occurred in a report of a match played on 6 June 1891, when Vivian was just three days past his twelfth birthday. The match was against Colchester Weslyans. Vivian opened the innings, scoring two runs. During the rest of the season he played regularly for the Ascham College First XI and gradually improved on that rather hesitant start. On 25 July 1891, it was reported that 'Woodward batted extremely well' in the match against Colchester Grammar School. In fact he was Ascham College's top scorer with 14 in the first innings and 32 not out in the second, again having opened the batting. His performance enabled Ascham to win by nine wickets.

To demonstrate his prowess as an all round sportsman, Vivian also took part in the Ascham College Athletic Sports Day in June of that year. He won both the under-13 120 yards and 440 yards events, earning himself 15/s in the process. His time for the 440 yards was 1 minute 12 seconds. This was possibly the first, last and only time that Vivian Woodward ever made any money out of sport.

At the end of year school prize day ceremony, Mr Wilson made a point of emphasising Ascham's sporting achievements: 'In the cricket matches we have won more than we have lost and our football teams were the strongest around. The first eleven has scored thirteen to nil and the second eleven has been equally successful.' In the course of his speech, he also made reference to the school's expertise at handiwork, citing in particular 'some pretty frames made by A.L. and V.J. Woodward.' Mr and Mrs Woodward were present in the hall and received further proof that Vivian's academic career had not been forgotten when he was awarded first prize for arithmetic. Alexander went one

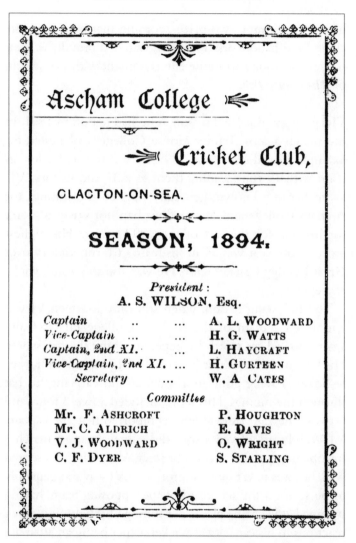

Ascham College
Cricket Club,
CLACTON-ON-SEA.

SEASON, 1894.

President :
A. S. WILSON, Esq.

Captain	...	A. L. WOODWARD
Vice-Captain	...	H. G. WATTS
Captain, 2nd XI.	...	L. HAYCRAFT
Vice-Captain, 2nd XI.	...	H. GURTEEN
Secretary	...	W. A CATES

Committee

Mr. F. ASHCROFT	P. HOUGHTON
Mr. C. ALDRICH	E. DAVIS
V. J. WOODWARD	O. WRIGHT
C. F. DYER	S. STARLING

Ascham College Cricket Club fixture list for the 1894 season, showing Vivian's brother, Alex, as captain and himself as a committee member at the age of just fourteen.

better by winning two prizes, coming first both in profi-
ciency and handiwork. They also watched proudly as their
son, Vivian, took part in the entertainment with a recitation
of *The Nancy Bell*.

Vivian began the 1892 season as he had left off in 1891. In
the match against Trinity House College, Colchester, for
example, played on 1 June 1892, he was top scorer for his
team with 19 runs, leading them to a 37-run victory. 'VJ',
as he became known, generally opened the innings for
Ascham College and more often than not was top scorer
for his side for the rest of the 1892 season. His highest
score of the year was 37 in his team's 61-run victory over
Great Bentley Cricket Club. He was also the team's wicketkeeper.

   The following season, when still only fourteen, VJ was
appointed captain of the Ascham College First XI and
again showed his worth by generally being the top scorer.
His best was 68 not out in a total of 154 against Thorpe-
le-Soken, having gone in as opener and carrying his bat
through the innings. This score included a five, 3 fours and
6 twos. The *East Essex Advertiser* reported that 'the captain,
V.J. Woodward, played a splendid game'. In most matches
his opening partner was his brother, Alex, who also scored
well, but was never quite as proficient. VJ was also generally
to be seen on the scorecard of the opposing team, having
stumped at least one player per innings; his lightning quick
reactions in his capacity as wicketkeeper being an attribute
that was generally to mark his future career in both cricket
and football.

   Having made such a fine start in his cricket career, his
father urged the young Vivian to stick with that sport as he

felt that football was far too rough and dangerous for the frail, dark-haired youngster. Vivian himself preferred football and tried to persuade his father to let him play. He was supported in his arguments by two teachers at the school, Messrs White and Knowles, who, having seen the young Vivian play in his very first match and run rings round his opponents, said to John Woodward that his boy 'will play for England one day'. His father reluctantly agreed and Vivian Woodward's football career began. In some ways, both his father and his two teachers were right. Woodward did, of course, go on to play for England, but he also suffered through the whole of his career because of his light build and was injured many times by unscrupulous players who, unable to deal with his speed and skill, resorted to dubious tactics, pushing him off the ball, hacking and kicking him. It was to be a recurrent theme at all levels.

The first mention of Vivian Woodward as a footballer occurred on 4 November 1893 in the *East Essex Advertiser & Clacton News* when he played at inside right for the strongest team Ascham College could put out, which even included some of the teachers. Vivian was just fourteen years old at the time. His brother, Alex, played at right half. The paper noted that 'the college subject themselves to a continual practice'. The result of this was that the college team were able to beat the Clacton Town Second XI with a 2-1 scoreline. Neither of the Woodwards scored. A few days later the two brothers turned out for Ascham College again, this time against a much stronger Colchester Second XI, who won 7-0.

At the end of 1893, Vivian proved once more that his academic career had not been affected by his sporting prowess as he gained a first division pass in the third class of the

College of Preceptors' Examination (perhaps best viewed as the GCSE equivalent of the time). Only six of the twenty-three entered for the exam gained a first division pass.

1894 saw VJ continue both his footballing and cricketing career at Ascham. In one memorable cricket match, played on 21 June that year, he scored 5 runs against St Osyth and managed to be his side's top scorer out of a grand total of 20. Needless to say, St Osyth ran out the victors (by four wickets).

The following week, however, the college team fared a little better as they managed to pack in three matches, winning them all, against Trinity College, Clacton Grammar School and Brightlingsea Second XI. VJ top scored in all three matches. At the end of the season he topped the school's batting averages with 31.0 and was presented with a cricket bag, bat and ball in recognition of his fine contribution to the team.

When the football season started, he was back in action. The first match of the season was against Colchester Town Second XI. Colchester, who were much more experienced, ran out 3-1 victors. The solitary Ascham goal was scored by Woodward with a superb header. This is the first mention of a headed goal by Woodward, but certainly not his last, as, over the years, this was to prove to be one of his many strengths. His height, light build and athletic ability seemed to give him an edge over most of the defenders he came up against and he was able to out jump them on a regular basis. Years later, referring to the fact that many of his goals at both club and international level came from his head, he was to say, 'It is easier to escape your policeman when the ball is in the air, especially if you are a couple of inches taller than they are.'

Vivian Woodward's first recorded hat-trick came on 14 November, when he scored three goals in a 5-1 victory over Clacton Grammar School. The local paper commented that 'Woodward's play is deserving of the highest praise'.

Towards the end of the 1894/95 season, VJ played at centre forward for a scratch team picked by Mr F. Davall, a leading member of the Clacton Town Football Club, against the Clacton Second XI. The match was played on the Ascham College Ground. The first goal was scored by Clacton Second XI but, on restarting, the scratch team took the ball straight down to the Clacton end by means of some good short passing, with the ball eventually finishing at the feet of Woodward, who banged in the equaliser. Twice more in the match VJ found the back of the net, and, although his team lost 6-4, it was clear to the management of Clacton Town Football Club that here was a youngster of exceptional talent. He was still only fifteen at the time and playing with and against players many years older than himself.

Woodward continued to play cricket for Ascham College, but it was becoming apparent that his real future lay in football. The 1895/96 season at Ascham opened with a match against 'Ascham Past'. Once again, the local paper picked out VJ for his performance, saying that 'V. Woodward played in his usual splendid style'. Clacton Town, meanwhile, had decided to take a step up and applied to enter the North Essex League Second Division. Until then they had only taken part in the Essex Junior Cup (a cup competition for non-league and lower league clubs) and a series of challenge matches. The application was accepted and Clacton, all set to move upwards and onwards on the football field, were looking round for more players to help them in their quest for honours. They had already pencilled in the young Woodward as a player to watch for the future, but when, on 24 October, he shot in five goals for Ascham College against Trinity College, the Clacton Town selectors decided that the future had arrived and they invited him to play for the Second XI in a challenge match against another local team called Old Clactonians. And so, on 2 November 1895, when still only sixteen, Vivian J. Woodward made his debut for a senior team, the Clacton Town Second XI. Not only did he make his debut, but he also scored his first goal for them, knocking in the second of the five scored by Town that day.

For the rest of November and early December, VJ continued to turn out for the Second XI. On 14 December he played in a special challenge match against the Clacton Town First Team. Although the First XI had no trouble in disposing of their reserves, winning, as they did, 8-1, it was noticeable that the young Woodward was the equal of his first team opponents. Consequently, he was invited to make his first team debut in a friendly against Manningtree the following week, on 21 December. The final score was 4-4. The *East Essex Advertiser & Clacton News* was fulsome in its praise for the new boy: 'As to individual play we will only refer to the importation into the first team in the person of V.J. Woodward. This was his first trial in the first team, and the general verdict on his play was most favourable. At the outset he was naturally a little reserved but as the game progressed he gained more confidence, and proved himself a valuable addition to the first team. His unselfish play was noticeable, and some of the older members of the team would do well to take a hint in this particular.'

The latter comment regarding his unselfish play was one that was to crop up again and again in Woodward's career as he proved himself a most generous and sporting player. Unfortunately it is not known whether he scored or not as no record survives of the goalscorers in that match.

Although he had played well, Vivian was not chosen for the following three league matches against Manningtree, Harwich and Parkeston and Chelmsford II and returned to the Second XI. On 8 February 1896, he took part in a match between Clacton Second XI and a team known as 'All Counties'. The match was held to raise funds for the Clacton Town Football Club and took on a novelty air as the Clacton Second XI played in top hats and the All Counties team in bonnets. In fact the match was advertised as Top Hats *v*. Bonnets. The two teams assembled at one of the town's leading hotels and marched behind the town band to the Recreation Ground where the match was to be played. Apparently, 'play proved very amusing, but it was generally conceded that the "Bonnets" were more heavily handicapped than their opponents who frequently broke the rules by taking their hats off when about to kick the ball…'

Woodward returned to the first team on 22 February and seems to have made all the difference to a team floundering in the doldrums at the time. The match against Bocking ended in victory for Clacton, 3-0, their first away victory of the season. In the first few minutes, Woodward got in two shots, the first just going wide, the second just over the bar, but he finally got his reward minutes before half-time when he netted the ball following a fine piece of combination play between himself and two of the other forwards, Almond and Owen. This was his first known goal for Clacton Town. At the beginning of the second half, Woodward once again just missed with a dangerous shot striking the upright. The ball was sent into Clacton's half of the field, eventually going for a goal kick. Clacton's goalkeeper kicked the ball out to Woodward who dribbled the ball up the field before some more passing play between the forwards led to a goal, this time from another Clacton forward, Turner. Shortly after the restart a foul was given against Bocking; the free-kick was hoofed up the field to Woodward waiting near the Bocking goal and this time he made no mistake as he knocked in his second and Clacton's third and final goal. The local paper's comment: 'Woodward played a sterling game as centre and proved himself a valuable acquisition to the team.'

At the age of sixteen, and still a schoolboy at Ascham College, Woodward now became the regular first choice centre forward for Clacton Town. On 7 March he recorded his maiden hat-trick for the first team, when he scored three goals in the 10-1 destruction of HMS *Mersey*, a warship stationed off Harwich.

At the start of the cricket season, Vivian helped to found a new club in Clacton called the Clacton Wanderers. Their first match was away to Great Bentley, who played their home matches on their village green, reputed to be the largest in Europe. The match had a very strange outcome as The Wanderers went in first and scored 125 for one wicket. At this point they declared, but Great Bentley refused to go in so the Clacton team just played out time, finishing with a total of 187 for 5, with Woodward contributing 44 not out to the total. He continued to play on and off for the Wanderers during the summer as well as for his school team.

At the Annual General Meeting of Clacton Town Football Club, Vivian's father, John, was elected a vice-president. The club secretary reported that the organisation had continued to grow and that there had been a marked advance during the season just gone of general interest and support throughout the town.

The opening match of the 1896/97 season was away to Manningtree. Clacton's first goal was scored by Woodward. The local paper reported, 'Woodward, who is in as good form as ever, soon began to bother the Manningtree half-backs, and by a pretty piece of passing on the part of the forwards, White centred the ball and Woodward shot for goal causing the home custodian to fist out. The ball fell at Woodward's feet and that player banged it into the net.' He followed this up with Clacton's second goal when he dribbled the ball past the backs and sent in a shot which completely baffled the goalkeeper. The final score was 3-1 to Clacton.

VJ seems to have scored a hatful of goals in his next match, but the local paper thought the contest too one-sided and dull to be worthy of much comment so it is unclear how many he contributed to Clacton's seven goal rout of Frinton FC, other than the fact he was 'responsible for most of them'.

Clacton's first big test of the season came on 14 November when they were up against Chelmsford Second XI. The last time the two teams had met, Chelmsford had run out 5-0 victors, but this time, with Woodward in the team, it was to prove to be a very different story. It looked at half-time as though this match might be going the same way, as Chelmsford led 1-0, but, not long after the resumption of play, some clever passing movements between the centre forward Beecham and Woodward – who in this match was playing at inside right – enabled the Clacton pair to get through the defence. The move ended with a pass from Beecham to Woodward, who put in a quick low shot which went into the back of the net, but was ruled offside. Although this 'goal' did not count, it was a sign of things to come in the second half as Beecham and Woodward continued to torment the Chelmsford defence. The final score was 2-1 to Clacton giving them a most unexpected victory.

Woodward surpassed himself in the following week's match against Maldon, which Clacton won 8-0. Woodward's unerring aim at goal resulted in a personal tally of five. There was no stopping Woodward or Clacton now. The next match, against Harwich & Parkeston II, resulted in a 10-0 victory for Clacton, with VJ scoring two and being instrumental in the moves that led to most of the others.

The first league match of 1897 saw Clacton away to Colchester Crown. 130 Clacton supporters availed themselves of Great Eastern's cheap day return issued specially for anyone going to the match. Woodward and Beecham once again combined well for Clacton, with some good passing runs up the field, but it wasn't enough for Clacton, who lost 2-0. This combination was once again to the fore in the match against Chelmsford II, but again to no avail, as Clacton again lost, this time 3-1.

Woodward's class was recognised by the Essex County FA, when he was chosen to play for his county in a representative match against Suffolk at Ipswich on 27 February, becoming the first Clacton player to be honoured in this way. (Although to be fair, it should be pointed out that the

Clacton full-back, Nightingale, was also chosen for Essex in the same match.) At this period county associations had much more power and authority than they do today and county matches were big occasions in the calendar, so to get the call to represent Essex was a big honour, especially for a seventeen year old. It should be remembered as well that Clacton Town were only in a junior league and there were a lot of bigger teams around in higher leagues such as Colchester Town, Ilford, Chelmsford, Harwich & Parkeston, Leyton and Leytonstone. Essex ran out victors in the match 3-1, with Woodward being responsible for one of the visitors' goals.

Woodward continued to play regularly for Clacton Town for the rest of the season, as well as captaining the Ascham College team on occasion. He continued to score in most matches for both teams.

During the summer he turned out again for Clacton Cricket Club First XI, but was no longer a regular player – although at the end of the season he was awarded a new cricket bat as a reward for recording the best batting average. At the end of the Ascham College Summer Term, at the age of eighteen, he left school. Like his father, and two elder brothers before him, Vivian went to London to train as an architect. For the next few years he divided his time between the two family homes at Clacton and Kennington and was thus not able to commit himself to playing full time for Clacton Town, though he did turn out as many times as he could, even commuting back from London especially for the match when necessary.

At the Annual General Meeting of the Football Club, held on 16 August, Vivian was elected to the club committee while his father was re-elected vice-president.

VJ's architectural training kept him away from Clacton for the rest of 1897 and he did not play again for the team until 8 January 1898, when he appeared as centre forward in the Essex Junior Cup third round tie against Colchester Crown in Colchester. Colchester won the match 4-0, but there were dark mutterings about a biased referee as, on one occasion, Woodward scored what seemed a perfectly good goal, which, to the utter dismay of the small band of Clacton supporters, was disallowed for offside. Not only that but this was the second time in the match that a Clacton 'goal' had been ruled invalid for such a reason.

There was better news for Clacton and Woodward in the next match, a league game against Chelmsford II, as VJ contributed two goals towards Clacton's 3-2 victory.

Towards the end of January, the local Clacton paper commented that Clacton Town had had a very unfortunate season and were now out of the cup and had little or no chance of taking any honours in the league. The reason for this was ascribed to the fact that the club was finding it very difficult to put out a settled team, as every match seemed to feature a different line up. Woodward's long absence at the beginning of the season had not helped. The season eventually stuttered to a halt with VJ managing to turn out in most of the remaining matches and scoring in most of those he did take part in.

He played more regularly for Clacton Cricket Club during the summer than he had the year before and was once again in splendid form. In the first match of the season he scored 67 not out in of a total of 128 against Tresidder Cricket Club; he also stumped two and caught one.

On 26 June he changed sides briefly as Clacton took on a combined Ascham College Past and Present XI. With Vivian in the Ascham line up were his elder brother Alexander and his younger brother Edward, who had followed his two brothers to the school. Clacton won the match 98 runs to 77, but Vivian was Ascham's top scorer with 30. VJ's good form continued throughout the summer and he was invariably Clacton's top scorer, making 37 against Saxon CC and 45 against Walton for example.

The Annual General Meeting of the Clacton Town Football Club was held on 15 August. The proposition that Mr John Woodward be offered the position of president was met with great acclamation and he accepted with due humility. His son, Vivian, was appointed vice-captain.

Back in active service on the football field, VJ soon made his presence felt, as in the second game of the season, against Long Melford on 1 October, he banged in five goals in an 8-0 rout. His fourth goal was particularly noteworthy in that he picked up the ball near his own goal line and ran practically the whole length of the pitch before knocking in a brilliant solo effort. In the next match, against Colchester Crown, he scored all three Clacton goals, once again one of them being the result of a fine solo run in which he managed to sidestep and elude the Colchester backs. Unbelievably, he completed a hat-trick of hat-tricks in the next match when he ran in another three goals in a 7-0 victory over Witham. Once again his second goal was the result of a brilliant run from the centre of the field. The subsequent opponents, Maldon, had clearly got the message and put a tight mark on Woodward. Although Clacton won 1-0, Vivian did not, for once, score.

In the next match, against Brightlingsea, he put in another of his individual runs, but this time was inadvertently robbed of the ball by one of his own side! Nevertheless he still managed to make his mark on the score chart with a beautiful shot, scoring the second goal in Clacton's 3-0 victory. It was the same story in the following match against Halstead. A 2-0 victory for Clacton with Woodward making a brilliant run for three-quarters of the length of the field, finally sending in a fierce shot which gave the goalkeeper no chance. In the next match, VJ scored two and made one of the four Clacton goals, giving them a 4-0 victory against Chelmsford Reserves.

The following game was a Junior Cup match against Manningtree. Once again Clacton proved the victors, this time with a 4-2 score. The first three goals all resulted from runs by Woodward who passed to Mansford to put the ball into the net. On 10 December, Woodward scored his fourth hat-trick of the season as he contributed three to the team's 8-0 win over Manningtree. By the end of the year, Clacton, under the influence of their inspirational centre forward, were unbeaten in league, cup and friendly matches. Their league record in particular was sensational: played 6, won 6; goals for 24, goals against 0. Of those goals, Woodward had scored ten.

1899 began where 1898 left off, with Vivian scoring a hat-trick in the first match of the year, bagging three goals in Clacton's 6-0 victory over Ipswich in a friendly. Unfortunately, shortly after this match, he fell ill and was unable to play again for the rest of the season. Although without his leadership in the front line Clacton couldn't keep up their unbeaten record, they held on well enough to finish the year as league champions. After the last match of the season, a home friendly against Parkeston Rangers, played on Clacton Recreation Ground on Easter Monday, a large crowd gathered in the centre of the field to witness the presentation of the North Essex League (Second Division) Championship Shield. It was a very proud president, John Woodward, who made a short speech congratulating the team, while an equally proud Mrs Woodward (Vivian's mother) made the actual presentation.

At the Annual General Meeting of the club, held on 7 August, Vivian was nominated to be captain. He declined the offer, saying that he felt it would be unfair for him to be captain as he would be away from Clacton for most of the week as his architect's training took place in London. In turn he proposed George Mathams (the same George Mathams who had come second in the three-legged race with his brother at the 1893 Clacton Regatta) for the honour. This was agreed and Woodward was then prevailed upon to continue in his role as vice-captain, which he readily agreed to do.

Although the club had come top of the league, promotion was not automatic and they remained in the Second Division for the following season. Unfortunately, VJ's business commitments kept him away from the team for the start of the 1899/1900 season. He was due to return on 20 January to play against Colchester Crown Reserves in the fourth round of the Essex Junior League, but on the morning of the match tragedy overtook the Woodward family, as his father, John, died at about 10.15 a.m. from a cerebral haemorrhage. He was only sixty years old.

As a result of the death of his father and his commitments in London, Vivian did not play again until 24 March, when he turned out for Clacton away at Harlow in the semi-final of the Essex Junior Cup and again on 31 March when he played in the Pearson Charity Cup final against Colchester. But it wasn't until 14 April that he managed to find the back of the net again, scoring the only goal in a 1-0 victory over Colchester Crown Reserves. On Easter Monday he played his part in a goal fest against Colchester Town Reserves, scoring two in the 9-0 win. The following Saturday, in the league match against Witham, he was again amongst the goals as he sent in such a fierce shot that the goalkeeper, in saving it, was injured and unable to stop the follow-up. Once again Clacton proved too good for the opposition, winning 3-1 away.

Although Clacton had not had a good start to the season, the return of Woodward proved a turning point in the team's fortunes and they once again went on to win the league, but this year they also added the Essex Junior Cup, thus completing the double. The final was played on 28 April against Barking at Witham. At first, with the wind at their backs, Barking were all over Clacton and after a few minutes went one up. This seemed to motivate the Seasiders and Woodward played the chief hand in getting his front line into proper working order and it was through him that the equaliser came. He got the ball in his own half and then dribbled through alone, but, with only the goalkeeper to beat, the referee blew for a foul committed by one of the Barking players off the ball. From the kick, the ball went to Woodward, he passed it to Pudney who drove it into the net. Despite playing into a strong wind, Clacton were now able to hold their own and got through to half-time with the score unaltered at 1-1. Clacton dominated the second half, with Woodward laying on a number of chances for his forwards, and although he did not score himself, he was instrumental in Clacton's final tally of three goals.

The news of Clacton's 3-1 victory in the final was tel-egraphed to Clacton and by the time the team arrived back on the train, the streets were already packed with supporters. Woodward and his fellow team members were placed in a waggonette and, headed by the town band play-ing 'See the Conquering Heroes Come', paraded through the town's principal streets to the Osborne Hotel, where a reception was held and the health of the team drunk.

The match that finally won Clacton the league title on goal average was much more decisive, if a little more con-troversial, as they clinched the shield by beating Earl's Colne 16-1. The runners-up, Colchester Crown Reserves, who would have taken the league if Clacton had not won by such a big margin, lodged an immediate objection and their case was investigated at a North Essex League committee meeting on 19 May. The grounds for their complaint were that the match should have been played at Earl's Colne but was switched to Clacton, that the visitors received more than their travelling expenses and that the referee for the match was not informed of the date of the match and another referee, appointed by the Clacton Town Secretary, officiated instead. Clacton's defence was that the original fixture was postponed and Earl's Colne had no ground available for the rearranged date, that, under league rules, the original referee should not take the match if the original had been postponed and that the expenses covered their railway fare, dinner and tea. The league ruled in Clacton's favour, but also considered the circumstances of the win warranted investigation and therefore returned Colchester's protest fee.

Woodward continued his cricketing activities for Clacton Town Cricket Club during the summer of 1900, once again playing a key role as leading batsman and wicketkeeper, but cricket was now definitely taking a back seat to football.

With the start of the 1900/01 season imminent, it was obvious that Woodward was playing a central and decisive role in the fortunes of Clacton Town Football Club. He had missed the latter part of the 1898/99 season and the team had fallen away. He had returned for the latter part of the 1899/1900 season and the team had picked up. He had led them from the front to two consecutive league wins and one cup win. His class was all too obvious and he was now being picked regularly to represent Essex at county level. Clacton knew that Woodward was destined for much better things than the North Essex League Second Division and they were afraid he would opt to leave them for a bigger club. An added problem was that Woodward no longer lived permanently in the town as his training had taken him up to the family's Kennington home. It was a worrying time for the Clacton Town team and its supporters but Woodward was never a man to let his fellows down and, as far as he was able, given his other commitments, he declared his loyalty to Clacton, pledging to stay with them for the 1900/01 season and to turn out for the side as often as he could. As a result of Woodward's pledge to play as often as he could for his home town team, Clacton took the plunge and applied for promotion to the North Essex League First Division.

Having been accepted, their first game in the senior league was away to Colchester Town on 29 September 1900. Although Colchester had the better of the first half, it was the visitors who drew first blood. The full-back, Rattee, passed to McKay, who, after dribbling some way up the field, passed the ball to Woodward who, after a splendid solo run, took a powerful straight kick at the goal which was too strong for the goalkeeper with the result that VJ had the honour of scoring Clacton's first goal in the North Essex League First Division. Colchester equalised just before half-time. At the start of the second half, Colchester were all over Clacton and quickly put three more into the Clacton net. Just after the third goal, however, the finest run of the afternoon was witnessed as Woodward took control of the ball, dodged four or five opponents and once again shot straight into the net. The final score was Colchester 7 Clacton 3. It was generally felt that Colchester were too powerful for the newly promoted Clacton team although the forwards, and Woodward in particular, played an excellent game.

There was some relief in the next game as Clacton took on the 12th Lancers in a friendly and won 6-1. At one point in the game, Woodward ran practically the whole length of the field, followed by four or five opponents, dribbling and playing one-twos off his team-mates. Unfortunately his final shot went wide.

The following week, Clacton were once more on the receiving end of a drubbing, this time from Harwich & Parkeston who beat them 9-1 in the Harwich Charity Cup. Following this match, Woodward was once more chosen to play for his county in a representative game against Middlesex on 22 November at Colchester.

Two days after the county match, Clacton found themselves up against Harwich & Parkeston again, this time in a league encounter. Having been annihilated three weeks previously by the same team, not much was expected from Clacton. Harwich & Parkeston were at this period one of the strongest amateur teams in the whole country not just

North Essex. They had reached the final of the FA Amateur Cup in 1899, just losing out to Stockton 1-0.

Clacton, on the other hand, were probably the weakest team in the First Division of the North Essex League. Another score of at least 9-1 was confidently predicted and expected by the Harwich supporters. Vivian Woodward, however, had other ideas. The *Clacton Graphic* reported that 'there was little to find fault with in Clacton's play... and much to praise. Each and every member of the team was on his best behaviour, but, of course, V. J. Woodward was the back-bone and centre of attraction in the team. Jack fairly eclipsed himself and waltzed round his opponents like a butterfly dodging a specimen hunter's net. The visitors were puzzled how to deal with such a slippery customer. They watched his every movement and endeavoured to frustrate every break, but it was of no avail, Woodward would get away, and when he found it impossible to shake his opponents off, he simply passed and re-appeared in another part of the field to receive the ball again. At last some of the Harwich team resorted to very questionable tricks.'

Woodward, however, had his revenge in the best way he knew how by scoring a hat-trick in Clacton's 4-2 victory. His second goal in particular was classic Woodward as he outplayed and bamboozled his opponents until near their goal when he sent a tricky shot straight into the back of the net.

Clacton's double gamble on applying for promotion and relying on Woodward commuting back for his team had appeared to pay off. After a hesitant start, the team had begun to gel and show it was capable of taking on the best. Woodward continued to show his true class by uniting and leading the side against one of the strongest teams at that level in the country in such a manner that they were able to defeat them.

Woodward's next match was another county game against Suffolk. Once again he was picked out for special mention, playing an 'especially good game' and proving himself to be a 'first-class county man'.

Clacton's next league match was another difficult fixture, this time away to Colchester Crown, but Woodward's second-half goal gave the visitors a 2-1 win. Clacton's first league match of 1901 was against Colchester Town. Town concentrated on marking Woodward out of the game, but even then they had to resort to foul tactics on a number of occasions, when Jack – as he was now universally known to his team-mates, supporters and the local paper – broke away and went on one of his individual runs. He scored Clacton's only goal in a 2-1 defeat. Strangely, Woodward's next two appearances on the football field were for Harwich & Parkeston. With a real chance of taking the FA Amateur Cup, Harwich 'borrowed' Jack for their first- and second-round ties against Marlow and the Old Etonians respectively. The score against the Old Etonians was 4-1, with Woodward contributing a hat-trick.

Woodward's exploits at county level and for Harwich & Parkeston in the Amateur Cup had brought him to the attention of the Tottenham Hotspur management. Tottenham, then in the Southern League, were strong contenders for the FA Cup and had reached the semi-final. It should be remembered that, at this time, all but one of the Football League teams in both Divisions One and Two (the only divisions then in existence), were Northern or Midlands teams – Woolwich Arsenal being the only exception to this rule. This meant that although the Southern League was slightly inferior to the Football League, it still represented the best of the London and Southern teams. Woodward was asked if he would like to have a trial for Spurs and was given a run in their reserve team.

With Tottenham due to meet West Bromwich Albion in the FA Cup semi-final on 8 April, they decided to rest most of their first team players on the Saturday before the big game and put out a reserve team – which included the young Vivian Woodward. And so it was that on 6 April 1901, at the age of twenty-one, he made his debut for the Tottenham Hotspur first team in a Southern League match against Bristol City. In their report of the match, the local paper, *The Tottenham Herald*, singled him out for attention saying he was 'a young amateur of promise'. And, although he was not mentioned by name in their report of the match, the other local paper, the *Tottenham & Stamford Hill Times*, praised him by implication, saying that 'It seemed that Bristol City would win easily at the start, but it was not to be, as the juniors pulled themselves together and infused an amount of dash and go into their work...'

With Spurs winning the Cup encounter with West Bromwich Albion, the management, in anticipation of the cup final itself, once again took the precaution of resting most of the first team players in the Western League match against Queen's Park Rangers on 15 April, meaning that Jack's services were called upon for a second time. This time the *Tottenham & Stamford Hill Times* did mention him, saying that he played 'in particularly bright fashion'. In fact, his play was so bright that he scored the first of the many goals that he was destined to score for the Spurs. He was also instrumental in Tottenham's second: 'A free-kick had been awarded them, and Tait placing it well in the goalmouth, a rare scrimmage ensued. Woodward cleverly kicked over the head of one of the opposing backs, Clutterbuck saved by falling half on the ball. He could not get it away however, and Jones, dashing up, put it into the net.' Scored one, made one. It was a sign of things to come! Once again the juniors acquitted themselves well as they drew at home with the full QPR team.

Woodward's next goals for the Tottenham Hotspur first team came on 27 April 1901, on the same day that the FA Cup final was being replayed after Spurs had drawn 2-2 with Sheffield United the previous Saturday. The match was a Southern League game against Gravesend, played in front of 4,000 spectators. In spite of having a reserve team out, Tottenham outclassed their opponents, winning 5-0, with two of those goals coming from the feet of V.J. Woodward.

Although he had no direct input into the Spurs Cup winning team of 1901, it is a fact that the Tottenham management were able to rest their top players safe in the knowledge that the reserves, including Woodward, would not disgrace the team. Indeed, they were even able to beat their opponents and win league points. So, in a very real sense, Woodward was an integral part of the Spurs effort that brought the cup back to White Hart Lane as the only non-League club (since the Football League was founded in 1888) to do so.

With Woodward fast becoming an established Tottenham Hotspur player, his appearances for Clacton Town were few and far between, as a result of which Clacton began to suffer both on the field and in falling support. At the

Annual General Meeting of the club held in June, the club secretary, Sid Thompson, began his report by saying, 'I am sorry not to be able to give such a flattering report as last year... We have had great difficulty in getting a fairly representative team together, two or three of our prominent players having, to all intents and purposes, left the town.' At the end of his report he announced that Clacton Football Club was over £27 in debt.

On 28 June 1901 another tragedy overtook the Woodward family as Vivian's eldest brother, Walter, died at the age of just thirty-three, leaving a widow and two children. VJ was present at his funeral, which took place at Christ Church Congregational Church in Clacton. Vivian felt the loss keenly as he was above all else a family man. He never got married himself, but was very close to his parents and his brothers and sisters and their families. He would visit them as often as his other commitments allowed and, later on, when his brothers and sisters started to have children, would spend hours playing football and cricket with them, patiently developing their skills, though he never allowed the games to become lessons. He knew that for the children, sports should be, above all else, fun. This, of course, very much reflected his own outlook on sport. In spite of reaching the very pinnacle of football fame, he never once looked on it as a chore. He was out to enjoy himself and he wanted to make sure his nieces and nephews felt the same.

Before the 1901/02 season started, the top two teams in the North Essex League First Division, Harwich & Parkeston and Colchester Town, both withdrew from the league, as a consequence of which it collapsed completely and Clacton were faced with no league matches for the coming season. With this, plus the fact that the club was already in debt and with the even more certain likelihood that Woodward would only play a very limited part in the following season, if at all, meant that Clacton Town FC temporarily folded.

TWO

TOTTENHAM HOTSPUR
AND ENGLAND
(1909-1909)

Although it now looked as though Vivian Woodward was bound for higher things as Tottenham Hotspur beckoned, he still wished to retain his association with the county of Essex. As playing for Clacton was now no longer an option, it looked at first as though he may move on to Colchester Town, but as they had withdrawn from the North Essex League, he decided to make a move to Chelmsford instead. Chelmsford had also been members of the North Essex League, but two seasons previously had transferred to the South Essex League. Woodward's move to Chelmsford allowed him to continue to play for the Essex county team, as he did on 2 October 1901 against Norfolk and on 20 November 1901 against Suffolk. He again showed his class in both matches. Against Norfolk, his last-minute dribble up the field and shot, which he cleverly placed in the corner of the net, allowed Essex to grab a last gasp 1-0 victory. Earlier in the match he had narrowly missed with an overhead scissors kick which the Norfolk goalkeeper was just able to fist away for a corner. As for the Suffolk match, *The Clacton Graphic*, still proud of their hometown son, summed up his performance with these words, 'Suffolk were troubled by a determined attack led by Jack Woodward, the brilliant Clactonian, and who is the Tottenham Hotspur reserve, and the new centre for Chelmsford.' Woodward scored Essex's second goal in a 3-2 victory that day.

Woodward's first match for his new club was on 21 September 1901 when Chelmsford opened their League programme for the season in a match against Ilford, holders of the London Senior Cup. Once again he scored on his debut, opening the home team's account with a clever shot into the back of the net following a fumble by the Ilford goalkeeper. It was generally agreed that Woodward's inclusion in the Chelmsford line-up as centre forward was a great success.

Woodward's reputation had already led to him receiving a rough ride at times at the hands of his opponents and his appearance as centre forward for Chelmsford away to Leytonstone at the end of November was no exception. He received a nasty kick almost on starting and from then on the home team hardly let up on him. Woodward, however, refused to retaliate. He saw no need for stooping to the level of his opponents and he was determined to show there was no need for it. By the end of the match he had even won over the Leytonstone supporters by his clever work and his skilful dribbling.

This was a theme that was to recur over and over again in Woodward's football career, but however hard the attention paid to him and however rough the tackling, he would never retaliate. And if sometimes his own team-mates wanted to step in on his behalf, Woodward would have none of it and told them to play the game cleanly.

Further League matches for Chelmsford followed: against Commercial Athletic he scored twice, both headed goals, while against Norwich C.E.Y.M.S. he didn't score but played his 'customary clever game'.

Meanwhile, Woodward was continuing to appear for Tottenham Reserves and, on the odd occasion, for the first team, as he did in a special representative match, Spurs *v*. Rest of the Southern League played in early October. He had a particularly good game for the reserves against Fulham in the London League on 15 November. Fulham had not lost in the League at the time and were favourites to retain their unbeaten record. Unfortunately for them they caught the Spurs Reserves at their most deadly as they crushed Fulham 8-2. In fact, the Spurs Reserve team for that match was exceptionally strong and would probably have beaten a number of Southern League first teams. Most of the reserve team players at that time were professionals, with only Rule, Gold and Woodward continuing to play as amateurs. But it was Woodward who was once again picked out as giving a 'fine display at inside right'. He scored one of his team's eight goals.

Woodward was to remain an amateur throughout his footballing days. He never even so much as claimed bus fares or other legitimate expenses. He was, of course, from a fairly wealthy upper-middle class family who never wanted for anything and he was himself training to be an architect and surveyor, just like his father and all three of his brothers. He had no intention of throwing all that up to become a professional footballer.

Interestingly, at about this time, the *Tottenham & Stamford Hill Times* carried a short piece about the changing nature of professionalism in football. Under the headline 'Football as a profession', it carried the following 'advice to juniors': 'Football as a profession is making great strides in popularity among the masses of today. A few years back professional football was only considered good enough for the poorest class, and for a man in a fair position to enter the ranks of the pro's – well, he was a fool, at least, that was the opinion of the majority of the south…'. The article went on to say that there had been big changes of recent date and now 'even' southerners were becoming professional footballers and it was no longer being seen exclusively as the prerogative of working-class northerners! The advice to juniors was that there was no longer any stigma attached to being a professional footballer and if they felt they were good enough there was no longer any reason not to enter football as a profession. In spite of the changing times, however, Woodward never felt the need to become a professional.

His last game of 1901 was in the Spurs first team when he 'played a sterling game' against Millwall in the Southern League. Although he had previously played on a number of occasions for the first team, this was the first time he was part of the strongest team Spurs could choose as, of course, his earlier appearances were due either to Tottenham's cup run and their wish to rest their top players, or in unimportant challenge matches. A lot of interest was therefore shown in how well he performed with the 'big boys' for the first time. The *Tottenham & Stamford Hill Times* reported that 'The amateur made his first Saturday appearance in the first team and a fine display he gave to, despite the big disadvantage he suffers through his lightness… Millwall scored first [but] the equalising goal was scored in the second half by Kirwan, who received [the ball] as a result of some clever play between Woodward and Cameron… The good show which Woodward made must have been very pleasing to the directors who showed great enterprise in placing a young inexperienced player (though a clever one) in the centre position against such formidable opponents as the Dockyard team…'

As 1902 dawned, there was much debate in the Tottenham camp about their forward line-up. Although the team had performed well to win the FA Cup the previous season, there was a feeling that the front line were becoming too easy-going and beginning to look very tired. It was felt that more desire and a bit of fire was needed. Many thought that if the old players were not capable of bringing about this change themselves then it was time for a new man up front to breathe life into the team.

During January and February, Spurs experimented with their forward line-up to bring about the changes needed. Woodward, of course, figured in these experiments, and by the end of February it was generally recognised that the man they needed to revive their failing fortunes was indeed V.J. Woodward. It was the Southern League match against Wellingborough that finally made up their minds for them. It wasn't just that he was a wonderful individual player himself, but at the still relatively young age of twenty-two he was able to inspire the whole team to new heights. Part of the report of the match emphasises this attribute: 'The talented young player, Woodward, officiated at inside right in such an able manner that by his efforts he brought about a wonderful improvement in the play of the front rank. The superiority of the home team was very marked throughout the whole ninety minutes, but especially so in the second half, when Woodward, Brown and Smith were continually bringing off brilliant pieces of combination that played sad havoc with the Wellingborough defence... Smith, judiciously fed by Woodward, put in several spirited runs that evoked great applause – applause that was well deserved, for such fine passing runs as Smith and Woodward treated the onlookers to on Saturday has not been seen for many a long day... The second half opened with a great save on the part of Clawley (the Spurs goalkeeper) [but] from this point until the close of play the ball was in the visitors' half of the field, and the game was a long succession of clever movements of the Spurs' forwards, the majority of which were initiated by Woodward... The third goal was the result of a clever and well-timed forward pass by Woodward that enabled Brown to break through the Wellingborough back line and put the ball out of Howe's reach into the net.'

The local paper's football columnist, 'Scorer', commented that the 'display given by the Spurs on Saturday last against Wellingborough augurs well... The improvement in the play of the front rank was very marked. The play of the amateur V.J. Woodward, was very fine, and on his play he is worthy of a permanent place in the team in the future. His style of play and dash is just the thing that is necessary at the present time to bring back the deadliness in front of goal which brought about such splendid victories last season in the Cup. His play on Saturday even had a marked effect on Brown, who, in the second half, was ever on the alert for forward passes and opportunities, the like of which have not come his way of late. Tom Smith also had more opportunities given him on Saturday than he has had for many a long day.'

It was obvious that Vivian Woodward had now arrived on the senior scene with a bang.

Shortly after this match, Woodward played in his first senior representative match when he was chosen to play for England in a Southern League 'international' on 7 April 1902. The match between England and Scotland was played on Tottenham's ground and was intended as a benefit game to raise money for the Southern League. However, the poor attendance meant that it turned out not to be as great a benefit as intended and only £54 was raised. The match itself was a good one, with Woodward playing a leading part in the England effort that day. Once again his key role was to ensure cohesion amongst the forwards and he was able to forge the England forward line into a unified whole and not just a collection of separate individual players. England's goal was scored by Cunliffe from a cleverly judged pass from Woodward.

As the 1901/02 season approached its end, the Spurs directors' thoughts turned to the line-up for the following season. Scorer offered them his thoughts on the subject:

'Woodward is looked upon as a certainty for next season's league team, and he is well worthy of his place. Several of his displays at Tottenham this year have been very clever. He has proved that he possesses ability far beyond the average. It is rarely that an amateur player can drop into a professional team's forward rank without upsetting the play of the line as a whole. G.O. Smith was one of the few amateurs who could manage this and Woodward is another. Not only has he taken up a position in the Spurs' forward line without disarranging the style of the game, but on the several occasions on which he has appeared has brought about a great improvement in the play of the front line.'

The telegram sent by Vivian Woodward's brother, Alex, to the family back in Clacton after his first international. It reads, 'England four Ireland nil Jack 2'.

G.O. Smith, to whom Scorer had compared Woodward, had been England's captain in the latter part of the nineteenth and early twentieth centuries, his last game in charge of England being on 3 March 1901. As centre forward he had netted 11 goals for his country in 20 matches. He had wonderful balance, timing and accuracy and though, like Woodward, he was slightly built, he was as hard as whipcord. He was reckoned at the time to be without peer in English football and was held in the same awe and reverence by the sporting public as they held for cricket's W.G. Grace. For a young amateur in his first season of senior league football to be compared to the great G.O. Smith was praise indeed.

In spite of such plaudits, and although now a regular first team player with Tottenham Hotspur, Woodward still found time to help out his Essex club Chelmsford when needed. For example, Woodward took his place at centre forward in the Chelmsford line-up in the quarter-finals of the Essex Senior Cup and was instrumental in helping his team beat South Weald to win the tie 4-2. His tricky runs, dribbling ability and fine passing with Frederick paved the way for the team's success. Oh yes, and he scored Chelmsford's last goal as well.

The semi-final was against Colchester Crown at the beginning of March and, once again, Woodward was there. He scored Chelmsford's first goal and held the forward line together. (In their previous League match without Woodward, Chelmsford had been beaten 6-0; the *Essex Herald* noted ruefully that 'Woodward's absence was severely felt'.) The final score was 2-2, which necessitated a replay. This time Chelmsford made no mistake and trounced Colchester Crown 7-0, Woodward scoring no less than five of them himself!

This victory put Chelmsford into the Essex Senior Cup final against Leytonstone. This was played on Easter Monday, 31 March 1902, at Ilford in front of a crowd estimated to be between 6,000 and 7,000, with 533 of those travelling by special train from Chelmsford. Once again Woodward forged his team into an unbeatable combination as they ran out 5-2 winners. This time he 'only' managed to score two himself.

Two South Essex League matches followed as firstly Chelmsford drew 2-2 with Leyton, both goals coming from the feet of VJ, and then against Leytonstone. This time, Chelmsford were unable to repeat their cup triumph with even Woodward unable to find the back of the net.

Woodward's last match for an Essex club that season was in the Pearson Charity Cup final, when, curiously, he turned out for Colchester Town against their local rivals, Colchester Crown. Although he scored for his adopted team for the day, Town came out on the wrong end of a 4-2 result.

At the Chelmsford FC annual dinner that year, the club chairman in his after dinner speech eulogised greatly about their star assets, Messrs Woodward and Frederick. The secretary, Mr J.E. Finer, responded by saying that but for Woodward and Frederick, he did not think the Essex Senior Cup would have come to Chelmsford.

Woodward's last match of the season was a special representative game between North Essex and South Essex played on 3 May in aid of the Ibrox Disaster Fund. The disaster had occurred on 5 April during a Scotland *v*. England international match; 68,000 people were present at the event. Not long after the start of the game, part of the terracing near the top gave way and spectators tumbled on to those on the lower terracing. In the ensuing panic, people on the lower part of the terraces tried to get away onto the pitch, but many were trampled on. In all there were twenty-five deaths as a result of the accident, with in excess of another 500 injured. The whole of British football went into mourning after the disaster and fundraising events were held all over the country to raise money for the victims and their families.

Woodward captained the North Essex side, with £11 14s being raised. At the end of the first half the score was North Essex 3 (Woodward having scored one) South Essex 1. In the second half the South Essex team ran riot and banged in seven goals. The *Essex Herald* commented that 'The North forwards seemed the smarter lot, but the right wing, instead of centring, persistently shot, and shot wide, when Woodward might have scored'. This seems to have been one of those rare occasions when Woodward was unable to stamp his authority on the game and mould the forward line into a single unit all working for each other rather than as individuals.

Although it now seemed certain that Woodward's future lay on the football field, he was still a great lover, and no mean performer, of the summer game and his skill at this sport was recognised by the Essex County side. On moving up to London in 1901, he had joined the Spencer Cricket & Lawn Tennis Club (see Chapter 7) and it was while playing cricket for them that he was spotted by the Essex selectors. In May 1902 he was chosen to play for Essex Second XI against Surrey Second XI at the Oval. He batted usefully and was second highest scorer for his team in the second innings with 21 runs out of a total of 131, helping Essex to win by 26 runs. However, he concentrated mainly on playing for the Spencer Club, though he did play one more good innings for Essex Club and Ground (a team which included first team players) against Colchester when he top-scored with 42 out of 134, helping his team win by an innings and 23 runs.

During the summer of 1902, Chelmsford Football Club held its AGM. The secretary reported that, in spite of missing a number of matches, Woodward was the team's second highest scorer with 23 goals to Frederick's 24. He went on to say that 'Much of the improvement in the team was due to V.J. Woodward, who sacrificed several opportunities of playing for Tottenham Hotspur first eleven in order to assist Chelmsford'. There was much applause at this.

Mr Finer went on to say that he was pleased to announce that 'Jack has signed up for another season with Chelmsford'. More applause.

For Vivian Woodward, the 1902/03 season started off where the last one had left out. His first game for Chelmsford was away to West Croydon on 27 September. Chelmsford thrashed their opponents 8-3, with Woodward scoring four. The *Essex Herald* noted that 'V.J. Woodward's re-appearance in the team had a marked effect'.

This was followed by another county match, this time against Suffolk. Essex won 5-3, with the forward line proving to be the better combination. Although he didn't score, he made a number of the Essex goals. The fifth was an especially good piece of work between him and his fellow Chelmsford forward, now also signed up for Spurs, Frederick.

For the next few weeks, Woodward alternated between playing for Chelmsford and Spurs. His first appearance of the season for Tottenham came on 13 October in a Western League match against Bristol Rovers. This was followed the following Saturday by a match for Chelmsford against Leyton in the South Essex League. The following week, he scored the third goal in Chelmsford's 6-3 victory over Halesworth in the FA Amateur Cup. Then it was back to Spurs on 8 November. Woodward played so well in this encounter with Portsmouth that there were grave fears in Chelmsford that he would now choose to play full-time for Tottenham. The local paper, *The Essex Herald*, ran an article in the following Tuesday's edition entitled, 'Woodward with the Spurs. Will he play regularly?' The article stated that: 'The match, Spurs *v*. Portsmouth, was played at Tottenham on Saturday before nearly 20,000 spectators. The interest from an Essex point of view was the appearance of Vivian Woodward, the popular Chelmsford centre forward, in a similar position for the Spurs. His inclusion was certainly justified, for, in the opinion of those who saw the game, he was the best forward on the field. It seems likely that the Spurs' manager will ask him to play regularly for the Tottenham team, which will mean a big loss to Chelmsford.'

For the time being, Chelmsford's fears were unfounded as Woodward did not forget his Essex roots. Later in November he played for Chelmsford in the next round of the Amateur Cup against Colchester Crown. Unfortunately, he was delayed reaching the ground and arrived late and came on to the field 10 minutes after the game had started. As he bounced onto the pitch, he was met by a loud cheer from all parts of the ground. As usual, he pulled the forward line together and Chelmsford were leading 3-1 when bad light stopped play. The replay was held on 30 November and resulted in a 0-0 draw. Woodward once again took his place in the team. In the meantime, he had also played for Essex as captain and centre forward in a county match against Norfolk. Unfortunately, Essex finished on the end of an 8-3 drubbing.

Following these matches, however, Woodward decided it really was time to make the step up and the Tottenham Hotspur board were able to announce that Vivian Woodward had agreed that he would play for them whenever required and it was 'convenient for him to play'. Spurs were in desperate need of a forward of the class of Woodward, as Sandy Brown had left the club during the summer. The loss of Brown was a big blow to the Spurs. He had scored 15 goals in the winning Cup run two seasons previously, scoring in every round. At Villa Park, he had scored all four of Tottenham's goals – including a memorable thirty-yard drive which completed his hat-trick. At the end of the 1902 season, however, he moved on to Middlesbrough and Spurs were in urgent need of finding a forward with similar talent. In Woodward, they were convinced they had got their man.

He played his first Southern League match of the season on 21 December, away at Millwall. The general opinion of his play was very satisfactory. He gave a fine display in spite of the disadvantage he suffered through his lightness, which the Millwall team tried to take advantage of but without success. Millwall scored first but the equalising goal came about following some clever passing play between Woodward and Cameron.

His last match of 1902 was on 27 December against Southampton in a Western League fixture. The final score was 0-0, but the general opinion was that Spurs and Woodward had been robbed of a perfectly good goal when he headed in and the Southampton goalkeeper, Robinson, fisted the ball out. Even many of the Saints' supporters felt the ball had crossed the line. The *Tottenham & Stamford Hill Times* summed up the general consensus when it said, 'It is at such moments that players and spectators feel something of bitterness towards referees.'

Although still a relative newcomer to the team, Woodward was appointed captain for the game against Bristol Rovers on 10 January 1903, in place of the regular captain, J.L. Jones, who was absent. His influence on the whole team was such that his appointment was a result of the other players choosing him as captain unanimously. Woodward celebrated his captaincy by scoring one of the goals in Spurs' 3-0 victory.

Towards the end of January, Woodward was chosen to play for the South in the International Trial. In the early years of the last century, the England team was chosen following a representative match played between the South and the North, which, effectively was between the Southern League and the Football League. Even in the relatively short time that Woodward had been playing top-class football, his skill had been recognised by the international selectors and here he was, the man who had started the season still playing for Chelmsford, on the verge of the big time and a possible international career.

The match itself was played on 24 January 1903. Although the North won 2-1, it was recognised that the goal of the game was the one scored by the South's centre forward, one Vivian J. Woodward, and it was regarded as the outcome of one of the finest pieces of forward combination imaginable. Such was the magnificence of the goal that, even before the match was over, the selectors had unanimously pencilled in the brilliant amateur at centre forward for the full England international team.

This was the first time that Woodward had really come before a national stage against a team composed entirely of the top Football League players. It is worth reproducing in full, therefore, the report of Vivian Woodward's role in the match as reported in the Lancashire newspaper the *Sporting Chronicle*, as it shows just what an impact he made on the game of football that day:

'This match was worth playing if it was only to discover Vivian J. Woodward, the centre of Tottenham Hotspur, who has now developed into the centre of England. Woodward is quite young, stands 5ft 10ins, and tips the beam at 11 stone. I should prefer him to be a little heavier, but weight will come. Born in the vicinity of Kennington Oval, he learned his football at a school in Clacton-on-Sea; but his experience in club play was limited to Chelmsford, and there Spurs found this amateur treasure. His form in the North and South match was a revelation to all the northern visitors, and, as a secretary to a leading [Football] League club remarked, he would like to put Woodward in his bag and take him away. With a subtle craft tucked away in his toes he combines most adroit head work, and between the two he opens out the game in dazzling style. Woodward is a great initiator, the personification of unselfishness, is quick to grasp the ever-changing situation of the game, and, above all, is "very cool".'

Woodward was now at the height of his footballing powers. He seemed to be able to do no wrong. On the Saturday following the representative match he was back in action again for Spurs in an FA Cup encounter against Bristol City. Part of the report in the paper the following week ran as follows, '…the ball was secured by Kirwan on the left, and negotiated to within 20 yards of the goal-line; when approached he swung it in to Woodward, who, in turn, baffled his opponents by passing on to Dryburgh; quick as thought the outside right returned it to his centre; and in a flash Woodward had shot into the net, and thus completed one of the most effective pieces of work seen on the ground this season. There was a tumultuous outburst of cheering; the crowd appeared to go frantic for a while with delight; and, as events turned out, the match was won… Woodward was the great cynosure of the afternoon, and his tireless energy and practically faultless style in dealing with the ball, were the admiration of everybody. His lithe figure was to be seen flitting from point to point with the dash and daring of a more seasoned player of heavier physique. How he tricked and eluded and outpaced his opponents could only be realised by those who witnessed the game; and it is safe to say that all his best qualities as a centre forward have not yet been discovered. It is sincerely hoped that he may continue in his immunity from injury at the hands of the vigilant and not over-scrupulous players who are told off to "mark" him.'

Woodward's international debut came on 14 February 1903, when he took on the role of centre forward for England against Ireland in front of 17,000 spectators (including his brother Alex), at Wolverhampton. Whether nerves got the better of him is uncertain but it is true that he started the match very tentatively and early in the game he missed an easy chance very badly. Gradually however, he began to make himself at home on the international stage just as he had done with every team he had ever played for and 20 minutes into the game he made amends for his earlier lapse. Passing smartly out to Lockett, he continued his run through the centre, received the ball back from the winger and guided the ball between the posts with a skilful left foot shot. Once again, Woodward had scored on his debut at a new level – this time the highest he could aspire to. Soon after the whistle blew for the start of the second half, Woodward had added a second to his and England's tally. He was denied his hat-trick shortly afterwards when a fierce shot at goal could only be parried by the Irish goalkeeper. The ball fell at the feet of England's inside right, John Sharp, who put in England's third. England finally won the match 4-0.

Woodward came in for his fair share of praise after his international debut. In its report of the match, the following day, *The Times* said that he had 'certainly added to the reputation he is making as a centre forward'.

Clacton, where most of his family still lived, had not forgotten their 'old boy' either and the local paper ran a piece eulogising about the former star of Ascham College and Clacton Town: 'As expected by his friends at Clacton, V.J. Woodward came out of his first international with flying colours. He was the only amateur playing on the English side against Ireland, and did more than his share in bringing about the result of 4-0 against Ireland. Jack not only scored the first two goals for England, but the third was secured by an opening made by him. Our young townsman has now been chosen to represent England against Wales, an honour he has richly earned.'

C.B. Fry, the legendary athlete, cricketer and international footballer, also put pen to paper in praise of Woodward, 'It must be very satisfactory to the selectors to find Woodward so great a success at centre forward, especially as he is likely to improve for several years to come, and will thus, perhaps, provide them with another "G.O.". At present I see not much likeness between Woodward and G.O. Smith. Indeed, the fact that they are both amateurs is about the full extent of the resemblance. But Woodward is a fine player who may become a great one, and he has a style of his own which is sufficiently good in itself… He is to be heartily congratulated on his success. It will be a surprise and a great disappointment now if he does not get his cap against Scotland.'

In fact, Woodward was one of only four players to keep his place in the England team for the next international, against Wales, on 3 March. This time the game was played at Portsmouth and resulted in another win for England, 2-1, with V.J. scoring the second and winning goal.

Already a success and establishing himself as a regular in the England team, it was the next international against Scotland on 4 April that put the matter beyond doubt. For the third time, he was the only amateur to be included in the full England line-up.

Following the match the newspapers lined up to extol his virtues. One typical report ran: 'Spurs' notable acquisition, V.J. Woodward, was for the third time in his initial international year doing duty as England's centre forward. That he has justified his selection beyond all reasonable expectations is shown by his achievement of having scored four of the seven goals obtained for England in the three matches, two against Ireland and one each against Wales and Scotland – a record which, as events have turned out, has secured the [Home International] Championship for England by virtue of goal average.'

This success, however, was not without its drawbacks as the nimbleness and speed of Woodward brought real problems to the opposition – problems they were unable to cope with in pure football terms and had to resort to more dubious methods. The report continued, 'During the generation or so over which international meetings have extended, there have been several similar instances of comparatively young players suddenly bursting into class brilliance – Linley and G.O. Smith being a couple in the same position as the Spurs' star; but the practice of "watching the man" has not always been so apparent or pronounced as in the case of Woodward. Naturally no player can be expected to stand aside and allow an opponent to romp

into his goal, but the tendency among modern professionals is in the direction of physical rather than tactical
opposition – regardless altogether of whether a man is
"laid out" and maimed or merely checkmated and pulled
up. This sort of recklessness is not often an element in
international matches – it is mostly imported into League
games in which points are at stake – but still on Saturday
Woodward was the object of attentions that were considered far too solicitous. He easily gave the go-by to his
vis-à-vis, Hamilton; but the Scottish halves and backs had
set themselves the duty of marking him; and the vigour
with which the men from o'er the Border executed some
of their movements was made clear by the number of fouls
given against Scotland.'

With the Home International season over, Woodward
returned to captain Tottenham in their last match of the
season against Nottingham Forest. Needless to say he
scored the two goals which gave Spurs their victory. It is
a remarkable fact that this was only Woodward's first full
season in Tottenham's colours, a season in which Spurs
did not lose a single League match in which Woodward
took part. At the still relatively young age of twenty-
three, Woodward had established himself as one of the
best footballers ever to don an England shirt – and this
in his first season of senior football. And yet Woodward
himself thought that one of his proudest achievements of
the season was gaining the Essex FA badge awarded to all
players appearing in six or more games for their county
in one season.

At the end of the season, football writer Alan R. Haig-
Brown contributed a chapter entitled 'The Leading
Amateurs of Season 1902-3' to a book about famous

footballers of the time, a book which carried as its frontis-
piece a photograph of Vivian Woodward. This is what he
had to say about VJ: 'Perhaps the name which was most
prominent in football circles during 1902-3 was that of
Vivian Woodward. G.O. Smith had taken his well-earned
laurel wreath into seclusion, and an anxious eye was being
cast round for his successor. Few thought he was to be
found among the ranks of amateurs until the Spurs brought
to light young Woodward, and England decided that what
was good enough for the London Cup-fighters was good
enough for her. He is a player with a great future before
him. Though built somewhat on the light side he is clever
and tricky, a master of the art of passing. It is a 1,000 pities
that his lack of weight renders him a temptation which the
occasionally unscrupulous half-back finds himself unable
to resist. His record of goals both in League matches and
in Internationals is a flattering one, for, all said and done,
the most important duty of a centre forward is to find the
net, and find it often.'

During the summer, he continued his cricketing career
with the Spencer Cricket Club, also finding time to turn
out for Essex Club & Ground (a team which included
the Essex First XI captain, C.J. Kortright, as well as other
first team players, H.G. Owen and Tremlin) and Essex
Second XI.

For the forthcoming football season, 1903/04, Woodward
once again signed amateur terms for both Chelmsford and
Spurs, but Chelmsford were under no illusions that they
would see their star centre forward other than on rare
occasions. His registration with Chelmsford, however, did
mean that he was able to continue to play for the county

team, as he did on 29 September against Norfolk and on 18 November, when Essex beat Suffolk 2-1 at Portman Road.

With the cricket season over, Woodward returned to the Tottenham line-up on 25 September. The local paper reported a much-improved attendance of 18,000 for the game against Plymouth Argyle: 'An explanation of the big attendance was to be found in the presence of V.J. Woodward at centre'. What had been feared for some time by Spurs, England and Woodward himself finally came true on 2 October when some over-zealous tackling put him out of action for several weeks. His return at the end of the month in a League match against Portsmouth was met with relief by the local paper, 'It is not often that the presence of one player has such a leavening effect in a team as is the case with the Spurs when V.J. Woodward turns out. This was strikingly shown on Saturday (31 October), and his fellow forwards emulated him in a manner that was simply irresistible.'

His next hat-trick came on 27 November when he put three past Brighton and led his team to a 7-0 drubbing of the south coast side. Woodward's following match for Spurs was against the Corinthians. The Corinthians had been founded in 1882 by N.L. Jackson. It was a strictly amateur club and was formed exclusively of ex-public school and university players. Right from their inception, they had been a very formidable team. For example, in 1884 they beat the great Blackburn Rovers by the massive score of 8-1 and this in the year that Blackburn won the FA Cup! In 1886, nine of England's international team came from the Corinthians, the other two being Blackburn players, while in 1894, the entire England squad that beat Wales

5-1 at Wrexham was composed of Corinthians. In 1904, the year following the Spurs match, they beat Bury 10-3, this being the same Bury team who won the FA Cup final that year by the record margin of 6-0 over Derby County. The Corinthians themselves never entered either League or Cup competitions. They were therefore a big draw at any ground they played at, and indeed, a larger than normal crowd turned out to see Tottenham *v*. the Corinthians on 12 December 1903. The attraction was made ever bigger by the fact that C.B. Fry turned out for them.

In spite of their undoubted skill and reputation, V.J. Woodward led his Spurs team to an incredible 5-0 victory, the *Tottenham & Stamford Hill Times* reporting that, 'One of the most notable features of the game was the ease with which Spurs romped round the speediest of opponents. This was especially the case with V.J. Woodward.' The appearance of C.B. Fry turned out to be something of an anti-climax as he was barracked mercilessly by the crowd for his frequent appeals to the referee over the most trivial of incidents.

Woodward continued in much the same vein into 1904. On 19 February, for example, he led Spurs to a 5-1 victory over Bristol City; Woodward leading the way by scoring goals one and two in the first 12 minutes – in spite of playing into a strong rain-laced wind.

Although now generally recognised as the best centre forward in the country, he was unaccountably dropped for the first Home International of the season against Wales, his place being taken by Sheffield United's Arthur Brown. Brown, however, had a poor match and Woodward was back in his rightful place for the next international, against Ireland, on 12 March. Although he played well, he did not score on this occasion – the first time he had failed to find the back of the net in an international game. Nevertheless, England still managed to win 3-1. VJ was selected for the final match of the Home International season against Scotland at Celtic Park. Once again he failed to score, the honour this time going to Steve Bloomer who scored England's only goal in the 1-0 victory. With 5 points under their belt, England ran out tournament victors once more.

Meanwhile, Tottenham Hotspur were riding high in the Southern and Western Leagues, finishing the season as runners up in the Southern League and winners of the Western League. The 1903/04 season therefore had been a highly successful one from Woodward's point of view – both individually and as far as the teams he played for were concerned.

Tottenham's prospect for the coming 1904/05 season looked good. They had a forward line the equal to any in the country, including Football League teams led and masterminded by the England international centre forward Woodward himself. As usual, he missed the first few games of the season due to his cricketing commitments, but he returned for the League match against Plymouth on 17 September. The local paper noted that 'the appearance of Woodward made all the difference, the smoothness of the machinery was apparent from start to finish, and the international centre delighted the crowd with his clever play'.

His next big challenge came in the Southern Charity Cup match away to Football League team Woolwich Arsenal. It almost goes without saying that he had another great game, feeding and keeping his wing together in magnificent style and leading his team with great judgment. Not only that but he also scored Tottenham's first two goals; the opening one being particularly memorable. Having received the ball from Brearly, he at once started for the goal with the Arsenal defenders in hot pursuit, but his pace was far too quick for them and he outran them; as he approached the goal, Ashcroft, the Arsenal goalkeeper came out to meet him but was unable to save the shot that Woodward placed brilliantly in the back of the net.

After this match, Woodward asked if he could be moved to inside right from centre forward. He thought that he was of more use to the team in this position. Although he had the ability to score plenty of goals – and did – he felt that his main role should be the brains of the outfit, keeping the forward line together, distributing the ball and generally trying to outwit the defence. His view was that he could do this better from the inside right position rather than at centre forward, where he felt there was more pressure on him just to score goals. He also felt that, as inside right, he would not face so many crunching tackles from burly full-backs intent on stopping him at all costs. He was proved right over the next few matches as he struck up a wonderful partnership with John Walton, the outside right. Walton, who came from Preston, was, like Woodward, tremendously fast and between them their passing runs down the right flank often left the opposition flat-footed and floundering. Many goals resulted from this deadly combination.

Probably the most perfect game Woodward, Walton and the rest of the forwards played that season was in the Southern Charity Cup final against West Ham early in the New Year. Spurs were in brilliant form. The second half in particular was a master class. Woodward had already scored one goal in the first half. Nine minutes after the start of the second, he added another. Shortly afterwards he took the ball in his own half and set out on a solo run carving his way through the Hammers' defence; with just the goalkeeper to beat he took unerring aim and there was Woodward's hat-trick. Minutes later he was off on another solo run, careering down the field, though this time from not quite so far back, but the ending was the same as he put in a shot that Kingsley, the West Ham custodian, had no earthly chance of saving. Four goals to Woodward. Near the end he added a fifth. With the other forwards also finding the five times, West Ham ended up on the wrong end of a double-figure beating. Woodward's dashing runs, deft passes, accurate marksmanship and natural skill as a footballer were a timely reminder to the England selectors not to overlook him for the forthcoming Home International tournament.

Woodward reinforced his claim to retain his place when Spurs took on a Football League team, Middlesbrough, in the FA Cup in February and drew on the latter's home ground. There was no doubt in the mind of the spectators that Woodward was by far the best forward on the field. In the replay at White Hart Lane, Tottenham knocked out their more illustrious opponents.

It was no surprise therefore when he was chosen to play his sixth international, against Ireland, at Middlesbrough on 25 February 1905. As it happens it wasn't a great game for him – nor for England who could only manage a 1-1 draw thanks to a Steve Bloomer goal – but he did enough to keep his place for the next international, against Wales, on 27 March. This time he played a much better game and, for the first time since his third international back on 4 April 1903, he scored. In fact he put two past the Welsh 'keeper, Leigh Roose, in a 3-0 victory for England. His performance in this match ensured his selection for the final international of the season against Scotland at Crystal Palace, which England won 1-0, the goal being scored by Aston Villa's inside left, Joseph Bache.

Because of his international commitments, he had missed a number of Spurs' games and his return was keenly awaited as Tottenham had not fared very well without him, losing to Swindon, Plymouth and Brentford. His return on 8 April resulted in a win for Spurs over New Brompton. In spite of this victory, *The Tottenham Herald* was not very impressed. Its report read, 'V.J. Woodward appeared in the centre for the first time for three or four weeks, but did nothing very wonderful'. Oh well, you can't win them all!

Shortly after this match Woodward went down with an unspecified ailment (which could explain why he did 'nothing very wonderful') and missed several more matches. For Spurs, the season was stuttering to an end. It had been a reasonable campaign without being spectacular as they finished fifth in the Southern League and eighth in the Western League, although they finished up in fine fashion by beating the newly crowned Southern League champions, Bristol Rovers, in the last match of the season.

After the close of the season, the Tottenham Hotspur team undertook a tour of Austria and Hungary. Because of his illness, Woodward left late and joined the team in Austria. Everton were also touring Austria at the same time, and after a 6-0 victory over Homen Wart Club, Vienna, Spurs and Everton met at the weekend in a special exhibition match in Vienna, with Spurs coming out on the losing end 2-0. Although it was only an exhibition match, Everton took the game very seriously and Woodward received a good deal of attention at the hands of their defenders, who fouled him continuously throughout the contest. The referee, Mr Barker, was very lenient and seldom blew up for any fouls, much to the disgust of the Tottenham players. After the match both teams were entertained to a banquet.

The following Monday the Spurs team were taken for a day out in the countryside by their hosts, the Vienna Club. There was a splendid picnic luncheon at which the English team entertained their Austrian hosts by singing a number of well-known English songs. After lunch they went for a ramble while Woodward indulged in one of his hobbies, taking many snap-shots with his new camera. It was a sign of the times that he was, in fact, the only one present with such a device.

Several more matches against local club sides were held, with Spurs beating the Vienna Athletic Club 4-1, Woodward scoring two; the Buda Pest Torna Club 7-1; Testgyakorborora 12-1, Woodward finding the net four times, and Slavia 8-1, with one from Woodward. They also met Everton in a second encounter, once again losing, this time by a single goal.

It was a pleasant and enjoyable interlude for the Spurs team and everywhere they went they were met with a hearty reception. The tour was a big success and they found a growing interest in football in the region: the teams they played, although not in the same class, were by no means humiliated. One problem they did find, however, was that the refereeing was not up to the standard of British refereeing and many fouls went unnoticed, leaving vulnerable players like Woodward for the most part unprotected.

A cartoon published in the 13 January 1905 edition of the *Tottenham Herald* to celebrate Spurs' 10-0 victory over West Ham.

Following this tour of Central Europe, Vivian Woodward was off yet again, this time with an amateur team calling itself the Pilgrims – essentially an all-star squad of top amateur English players – for a first-ever visit by a British team to Canada and the USA.

The tour started in Canada, where the Pilgrims played in Montreal, Hamilton, Niagara Falls, Berlin and finally against the unofficial 1904 Olympic Champions, Galt, in front of a 4,000-strong crowd. This latter match was billed as for the 'Championship of the World' and finished in a 3-3 draw. The team then moved on to the USA, where they played another twelve games against teams such as Chicago All-Stars, to whom they suffered their only defeat of the tour, Boston and St Louis.

The Pilgrims found themselves in great favour with President Theodore Roosevelt, who was conducting a campaign to eliminate brutality from American college football. The idea of inviting the Pilgrims in the first place was to popularise soccer in the United States, and before they returned to England, Woodward, together with the Pilgrims' captain Fred Milne, were invited by the president to visit the White House, for a discussion of the sport.

In fact, the visit of the Pilgrims to North America in 1905 represented the first serious attempt to popularise soccer with the American public, and Milne underlined the team's mission in an interview with *The New York Times* when he said, 'We came to America to demonstrate Association Football as it is played in England. We heard that the game was not generally played in the United States. Our idea was to come over and start a boom for it, which would result in popularising it and produce teams which would visit England for international play.'

Woodward came back to Tottenham for his usual late start to the season, by which time the team had made a good start with six wins, two draws and two losses. Woodward returned in time to add a seventh win with the only goal of the match in a 1-0 defeat of Luton in front of 22,000 spectators at White Hart Lane, by far the biggest crowd of the season so far. It was a tribute to Woodward's skill and his contribution to the team that his appearance on the field usually put several thousands on the gate.

In the early part of 1906, Woodward went through the normal preliminary stages of the Home International selection procedure. He played well in the Amateur *v.* Professional fixture and then again in the North *v.* South match at Leeds on 22 January, scoring one of the two goals which gave the South victory. Unfortunately, he was badly injured in the North *v.* South match and was unable to play again until 24 February, when he turned out for a cup tie against Birmingham in which he was promptly injured again and was out for several more weeks. His injury meant that he missed all three of the Home International games and he did not return to active football until 31 March, in a Southern League match away at Northampton. With his long absence, Spurs had already given up their chance of the League title but they did well to maintain their fifth place in the table.

Woodward returned for the 1906/07 season for Spurs' fifth Southern League match (against Norwich City). At this point, they had won one, lost one and drawn two. With his return, Tottenham went unbeaten for the next six matches. By 12 October they had gone to the top of the League. The *Tottenham Herald* had no doubt who was responsible for this change in fortune and the rise to first place: 'After an indifferent beginning the Spurs ended the first month in a blaze of glory, and at present moment they are perhaps the most respected team in the Southern League... The introduction of V.J. Woodward has had a most beneficial effect, he is not to be surpassed at affording opportunities for others. He has pulled the forwards together, and the team has brightened up all round.' When he missed a Western League match on 20 October, the forwards put up a comparatively tame showing. Once again the *Tottenham Herald* knew why this was: 'The forwards needed the inspiring assistance of V.J. Woodward, to whose initiative they often owe a great deal.'

His contribution to the team's performance had not gone unnoticed by the other sides and they were still determined to stop him at all costs. Spurs Southern League match against Fulham at Craven Cottage on 29 October was a particularly nasty example of what some of the other teams felt they needed to do to combat Woodward's skill and command of the pitch. Two players in particular, Ross and Morrison, were strongly condemned by the sporting press after the match for the way they set about Woodward. He was kicked and pushed both inside and outside the penalty area and it was a wonder that he was not seriously injured again. There were many calls for this sort of behaviour to be dealt with more severely by the referee and the football authorities.

In spite of the attention he received, Woodward was not badly hurt. This was just as well as three days later he was due to play in England's first-ever amateur international against foreign opposition. This had been organised following a split between some of the amateur associations and clubs and football's governing body in this country, the Football Association. The split arose from a resolution which had been passed by the Football Association which said that County Associations should permit the affiliation of all-professional organisations within their area. Most County FAs could see nothing wrong with this, but to clubs in and around London this was an anathema as they felt that professionalism was ruining the game. Consequently, in the summer of 1906, Surrey and Middlesex County FAs and some of the London amateur clubs organised a campaign against the new rule and formed the Amateur Football Defence Federation. The Football Association immediately outlawed any club belonging to the Federation, which retaliated by forming their own Amateur Football Association. There was very little support for their position outside the London area and even within it many players and clubs remained faithful to the Football Association, including the great amateur himself, Vivian Woodward. He had been playing alongside professionals for five years now and saw nothing wrong with the FA's original proposal.

With FIFA having been founded in 1904 and now recognised as the governing body for the sport throughout the world, their support for one of their affiliates, the English FA, proved crucial and messages of support for the official position were received from the FAs of France, Holland, Austria, Germany, Hungary, Denmark, Belgium and Bohemia. In order to reinforce the message that they were the official governing body for amateur football as well as professional football in this country, the FA organised an amateur international match against France and chose the team.

To prove they meant business, the FA selected their strongest possible eleven. Five of them were full England

internationals, including the three inside forwards –
Woodward, Sam Day and the current England captain, Stan
Harris. As it turned out this proved to be a bit of overkill
and led to a very one-sided match, particularly as these
three scored 13 goals between them.

Unfortunately there seems to be some discrepancy as to
exactly how one-sided the match was, with *The Times* and
the *Sporting Life* in their reports of the match the following
day giving the final score as 16-0 while the FIFA official
record shows it as 15-0. There is an even bigger discrepancy
over who actually scored the goals as *The Times* and the
Sporting Life gave the goalscorers as: Woodward 8, Day 3,
Harris 2 and one each for Robert Hawkes, P. Farnfield
and J.E. Raine; the official FIFA record showing them as
Harris 7, Woodward 4, Day 2 and one apiece for Raine
and Farnfield. Depending on which version is correct, it
means that either Woodward or Harris holds the record for
the most number of goals scored by an England player in
an international match – amateur or full.

Woodward's next amateur international match was a
little nearer home and certainly against a much stronger
team as England took on the Irish amateurs in Dublin on
15 December. This time England just scraped through 2-1.

Back in the Southern League, Spurs were just about
holding their own, winning and losing matches in equal
numbers. Between 10 November and the end of 1906 they
won four and lost four. Woodward had missed a number
of these, both through his international commitment in
Dublin and his usual Christmas break, when he preferred
to visit his family in Clacton rather than play in all three
games over that period. But Tottenham's fortunes began
to look up on 5 January when Woodward took a decisive

hand in a 4-0 beating of Bristol Rovers, the great man contributing two to the total and completely dominating the centre of the field. His first goal in particular was a beauty as he headed the ball in at what seemed an impossible angle giving the goalkeeper no chance. However, in an FA Cup match against Hull City on 17 January, Woodward was injured and, although at first sight the injury did not appear to be too serious, it turned out that he had suffered a severe blow to the upper part of his leg which caused extensive swelling. The doctor ordered complete rest and confined him to bed. It meant that not only did he miss several Spurs games but also the South *v.* North International Trial.

While he was off, a rumour circulated, and was reported in several of the national daily papers, that he intended to retire from football at the end of the current season. This was backed up by the view in some of the papers that Woodward was sympathetic to the position of the breakaway Amateur Football Association and that that was why he was going to retire. Woodward himself lost no time in contradicting the reports and issued a very terse statement to the press merely saying: 'Statement, as usual, without foundation.'

Woodward returned to the fray for a third round FA Cup tie against Football League team Notts County on 23 February 1907. It was not a happy day for Tottenham as they lost 4-0. Woodward himself was not yet back to proper match fitness and did not play as well as he could have. In fact, there was some talk in the national newspapers that perhaps Woodward's great days were over. On 23 March *The Times* had this to say about him, 'The [England] selection committee have not yet succeeded in finding a satisfactory set of forwards, the want of a really competent centre forward being the great difficulty. There is always V.J. Woodward to fall back upon; but there is no denying that he has lost a little of his pace, and is more easily knocked off the ball than was the case last year – as a result, it may well be, of the drastic treatment which has been meted out to him by unscrupulous defenders in the rough-and-tumble of Southern League football.' Even the *Tottenham Herald* made the point that 'The spectators [at the Notts County game] were disappointed in him. We heard him being discussed in a crowded tramcar after the match, and the opinion was expressed that he was an overrated player.' However, the *Herald* urged Woodward to ignore this judgement as they felt his dip in form was just a temporary blip due to his recent enforced lay-off.

It took him a few matches to get back into his stride and it was not really until the match against New Brompton on 16 March that his clever and decisive contribution to Spurs' 2-0 victory was what the fans had come to expect of him.

On 1 April, Woodward was back in action for the England amateur international team, this time against Holland in The Hague. An impressive 8,000 spectators watched the match – a record for any football match in Holland at that time. Although the Dutch amateurs were not quite as weak as the French, it was still a very one-sided game as England ran out 8-1 victors, Woodward finding the net once.

By the time of the Easter League programme, Woodward was back to his absolute best: the Good Friday game against Southampton being a classic example. Spurs' 2-0 victory was due in no small measure to his brilliance as once again he bewildered his opponents with his fast runs and accurate passes.

Having missed the first two games of the Home International season, Woodward's return to form saw him selected to play as centre forward in the final match of the tournament against Scotland at Newcastle, in the match which was to prove to be Steve Bloomer's last international appearance. Fittingly, it was Bloomer who scored England's only goal in the 1-1 draw.

Once again Spurs were just outside the honours in the Southern League as they finished sixth, but they did finish the campaign on a high note as, in their last match of the season, they took the Southern Charity Cup, beating Southampton 2-0 in the final. Woodward was once again picked out as the best of the forward line, though there was actually some criticism that he had been too unselfish and maybe should have tried a few more shots himself instead of passing to his colleagues. Nevertheless at the end of the match the 10,000-strong crowd surged round the stand where the well-known musical comedy actress, Edna May, was seated ready to make the presentations. She made a short speech and then handed out the medals. As she gave each Tottenham player his medal there was a big round of applause, with Woodward clearly receiving more prolonged applause and louder cheers than the rest.

At the end of the season, Tottenham undertook a short tour of Belgium, playing Fulham in an exhibition match, winning 2-1 and then taking on local side Ostend, beating them 8-1 with Woodward scoring two of the goals.

As usual, Woodward returned late for the 1907/08 season. On 6 September the press even went so far as to announce that 'V.J. Woodward will remain faithful to cricket and tennis for a little longer, and therefore will not turn out for the

Spurs just yet.' In fact, although he did not play, Woodward was present for the first home match of the season against Bristol Rovers in his new capacity as a director at Tottenham Hotspur Football Club, a position to which he had been appointed during the summer. No doubt he was very pleased by what he saw, as Spurs won the Western League match 10-0. He continued to attend in his capacity as director until he finally made it to the pitch on 5 October in a Southern League game against Crystal Palace. After a good start to the season, being unbeaten in their first three home matches, much was expected of the Tottenham team with the return of Woodward. Unfortunately for once he did not play well and Spurs lost their unbeaten home run 2-1. The supporters excused him on the grounds that it was his first match of the season and he was not quite up to full fitness yet. There did not seem to be much improvement over the next two matches, against Luton and Brighton, but at last, on 26 October, the old Woodward seemed to return and he helped his team to a 2-1 victory away at Portsmouth.

There was some controversy at the match with Millwall on 9 November as Woodward scored both goals in Spurs' 2-1 victory. Millwall complained long and loud that the ball did not cross the line for the first 'goal'. Woodward himself declared that it did and that was good enough for the referee as it was well known that Woodward would not cheat. The Millwall crowd thought otherwise and kept up a vociferous barrage of Woodward and the referee.

Woodward's good form continued. His command of the ball and his leadership were as outstanding as ever and his inspired right-side partnership with Walton, who was also in excellent form, was the main reason why Spurs remained unbeaten in the League for five matches through

October and November. It came as a blow to Spurs when Woodward was chosen to play for England in an amateur international against Ireland, thereby missing their away match at Reading.

A crowd of 10,000 turned out to see the international at White Hart Lane. Ireland started well, but a mistake by Foye, the Irish goalkeeper, after 20 minutes let Woodward in to score an opportunist goal and from then on England gained the upper hand with Woodward the motivating force behind attack after attack. Although he scored no more himself, he was the inspiration for all five of England's subsequent goals in their 6-1 victory. Meanwhile, without him, Spurs suffered a 3-1 reverse at Reading.

A 5-1 victory over Watford in Tottenham's next match showed that Woodward was back to his accustomed position in the Spurs forward line, this time netting two goals himself.

On 21 December, he was chosen to captain the England amateur side against Holland at Darlington. It was a very one-sided affair. Woodward, playing at inside right, opened the scoring for England less than a minute after the whistle had blown to start the game and, by the end of the first quarter of an hour, two more had been added by the centre forward, H. Stapley, and the inside left, A.A. Bell. Two more goals came before half-time, Woodward scoring the fifth. The change of ends brought no relief to the Dutch as England finally ran out 12-2 winners, Woodward adding a third to complete his hat-trick.

For the first time in many years, Woodward did not visit his family in Clacton at Christmas, preferring instead to make himself available for his team over the holiday fixtures. On Christmas Day he knocked in both of Tottenham's goals in the

2-0 defeat of Northampton Town. Summing up his contribution to the team over the Christmas period, the *Tottenham Herald* opined that 'Woodward's value to the Spurs seems to increase with every match. On Wednesday [25 December] he was again the chief figure in the home front line, and he is adding to his reputation by scoring goals, eleven in his last four matches. If England can find a better centre than he for the principal Internationals it will be surprising.'

Early in the New Year (1908), the Tottenham team were taken off to Southend to put in some training by the seaside in preparation for their FA Cup tie against Everton. Interestingly, Woodward did not attend the training sessions as a player, but looked in one evening as a director, along with one or two other directors. Unfortunately for Spurs the extra training was not enough for them to stave off a 1-0 defeat at the hands of their Merseyside opponents.

Later in January, Spurs met Swindon in a League match, which Woodward missed. His reason for not playing was put down to 'wishing to rest before the forthcoming South *v.* North international trial.' Local opinion was not so sure. There was a feeling that he had deliberately missed the match as he did not wish to pit himself against the Swindon centre half, Charlie Bannister. In the event it appeared that Woodward was right to be dubious about playing against Swindon as there were a number of unpleasant incidents during the match as the half-back line in general – and Bannister in particular – indulged in improper tactics.

Having saved himself for the international trial, Woodward put on a splendid display and booked himself a certain place in the forthcoming internationals, the selection committee preferring to play him at inside right rather than centre forward.

On 7 February came the news that Queen's Park Rangers intended to apply for admission to the Second Division of the English Football League. With Fulham having defected the year before to join Arsenal and Chelsea, it gave the Tottenham directors plenty to think about. With most of the top London teams playing in the Football League rather than the Southern League, Tottenham would soon be relegated to a second class club – not a happy position for a team that had for many years been seen as one of the top London sides.

The first match of the Home International Championship was played on 5 February against Ireland in Belfast. Not only was Woodward confirmed in the role of inside right, but, for the first time in his career, was given the great honour of captaining his country. He celebrated his achievement by leading his men to a 3-1 victory, scoring the second goal himself. The match was a triumph for him and the England selectors were more than pleased with his performance, both as a player and as captain. But if they thought that performance was good, even better was to come in the next international against Wales on 16 March at Wrexham. This one resulted in a 7-1 win for England, with Woodward picking up a hat-trick. It was not quite the same story in the last international of the season as England were held to a 1-1 draw by Scotland at Hampden Park. Nevertheless, Woodward had led his team to a joint share, with Scotland, of the Home International Championship.

While the Home International tournament was going on, Woodward also found time to captain the England amateur team in a return match against France at Park Royal. The French performance was little improved from their first match with the English, losing 12-0 this time. Woodward, playing at inside right, scored a hat-trick. Shortly after the match against Scotland, there was another amateur international, this time away to Belgium. The result was an 8-2 victory, with Woodward scoring his third consecutive hat-trick in an amateur international. Two days later he was in Berlin captaining the side against Germany. A crowd of 5,000 – the largest ever recorded in Germany for a football match at that time – witnessed another excellent performance by the English team, in particular the forward line. This time, Woodward failed to make a hat-trick, scoring two in the 5-1 victory.

These constant calls on Woodward's services in both full and amateur internationals meant that he missed a lot of Spurs' end of season matches, with the result that Tottenham won just four out of their last ten fixtures. There was some feeling locally that the Football Association ought to consider this problem for next season and either that internationals should be played on days when there was no league programme or that teams with internationals playing should be allowed to postpone their game. The Spurs directors were urged to take the matter up with the FA.

Strangely, Woodward did find time to play in one match for Spurs Reserves on 14 March against a representative team from the local Tottenham League & Alliance. His appearance in this match was due to the fact that his younger brother, Edward, who had followed his elder brother's footsteps by appearing for Clacton Town, was being given a trial for Spurs Reserves in this game at outside left and Vivian wanted to partner him at inside left. Edward was very nervous and, apart from one good movement with his brother which took them from the halfway line to their opponent's goal, did not show to any great advantage.

Following discussions within the club, the directors finally agreed to join Queen's Park Rangers and Bradford Park Avenue in applying for membership of the English Football League Second Division. Towards the end of March a special meeting of the Southern League was held at which all three teams were asked to hand in their resignation from the Southern League if they intended to proceed with their applications. The Tottenham management made a formal protest that the resolution was invalid; they were concerned that they could resign from the Southern League but not be accepted into the Football League and would therefore have no senior football at all in 1908/09. However, their motion that the resolution was invalid was also voted on and their protest was lost.

As it happened, they were right to be worried as their original application to join the Football League was not accepted and they faced the worrying prospect of no League football in 1908. Fortunately, at the last minute, Stoke withdrew from the League and Tottenham took their place by the chair's casting vote. It had been a close thing, but on 1 September 1908 a whole new era opened up for them and Spurs played their first match in the Football League against Wolverhampton Wanderers.

Woodward had, of course, been away in Austria–Hungary over the summer (see chapter eight) and had returned as normal to take up his cricket bat and tennis racket with the Spencer Club. A trial match was held at Tottenham prior to the commencement of the season in which he did not play, saying that he intended, as he had done every other season, to continue playing cricket until 12 September and that he would return to football after that.

However, the lure of playing in Spurs' first-ever Football League match proved too much for him and he decided to take part at inside right in the match against Wolves after all. Although in the Second Division, Wolverhampton were the FA Cup holders and one of the best teams in the division. It was felt that Spurs had been given a hard match for their debut, but their decisive victory over the cup-holders showed that Tottenham had nothing to fear from any team at this higher level.

Right from the start, Spurs played the better football, the forwards being well supported by their half-back line – who were working together so well that it seemed as if the summer break had never happened. The result of this combination was a series of attacks on the Wolves' goal. During one of these forays, the Wolverhampton goal-keeper, Lunn, made the mistake of carrying the ball out-side his area. The resulting free-kick was taken by Walton, who fired in a tremendous shot which Lunn could only parry. The ball fell at Woodward's feet and he made no mistake. The ball was in the back of the net. After just six minutes, Vivian Woodward had scored Spurs' first-ever Football League goal. The crowd went wild with excite-ment: the cheers echoed all round the ground and could probably be heard over most of Tottenham. It was a great and significant moment for the club and once again it was Woodward, with the help of John Walton, who had been responsible for it.

During the rest of the first half Woodward and Walton continued to torment the Wolves' defence but there was no more scoring, though both had goals disallowed for offside. The second half started off with an attack by the Spurs' forwards, the ball came across from the left wing to Walton on the right, who crossed it in to Woodward and bang – there was goal number two for Woodward and Tottenham. The one-sided contest continued. Shortly after the restart from the goal, Woodward gained possession of the ball and dribbled his way round three opponents, finishing with a clever, though not quite accurate, shot. Lunn then brought off a brilliant save from Woodward. The third goal eventually came from a half-back, Tom Morris, who sent in a long awkward shot from at least 30 yards out, the ball sailing under the crossbar and between Lunn's outstretched hands.

The 3-0 result was a triumph for the Spurs. Woodward had yet again shown his mastery of the game. His remarkable control over the ball, his leadership qualities and his fitness – even after the summer break – were instrumental in the victory which very few people had given his team the chance of pulling off before the match. There is no doubt that, at the age of twenty-nine, he was now playing some of the best football of his career.

After this match, Woodward returned to cricket for the next few Saturdays, finding time to return to the football fray FOR just one midweek match on 12 September when Tottenham took on and beat Barnsley 4-0, Woodward contributing one goal and creating the chances for the others. His Saturday return came on 3 October against Derby County in a 0-0 draw. In the meantime he had been chosen to play in a representative match for the Football League against the Irish League, being the only non-First Division player to be picked.

Woodward missed a number of matches in October as he was captaining the Great Britain side at the Olympic Games (see chapter eleven), but he returned at the end of the month for a game against Stockport County, another 0-0 draw. Spurs distinguished themselves on 14 November when they won 4-0 against Birmingham in a one-sided match. Woodward reverted to the centre forward position and put two goals past the Birmingham goalkeeper. It was felt that this was now probably his best position and, with one or two exceptions, he remained at centre forward for the rest of the season.

With Woodward now back more or less permanently in the side, they entered a purple patch, winning six matches on the trot, during which period Woodward scored seven goals. The run came to an end at the Christmas Day fixture away to Oldham. Woodward was in Clacton!

He came back for the return match the following day, but it was almost a disaster. The attendance exceeded all expectations and there was such a rush just prior to kick-off that the turnstiles were unable to cope. Shortly after play actually started, the pair of wooden gates to the left of the turnstiles were forced open and several thousand people swarmed in without paying. Additional police were drafted in and they managed to get the outer gates closed to prevent even more people getting in. The referee, Mr Howcroft, stopped the game for several minutes while the people inside the ground were spread out so as to avoid a big crush at one end. Although unfortunately one man died as a result of the incident, the consequences could have been far worse.

After this, play started rather hesitantly and there was no score at the end of the first half. But Spurs livened

up after the interval and, in a move reminiscent of their
first-ever League goal, Walton took a fierce shot which the
Oldham goalkeeper, Matthews, pushed out to the feet of
Woodward who returned the ball straight into the net: 1-0.
Bert Middlemiss added a second and then, in a move similar
to the first goal, Woodward tried to turn the ball into the
net from a centre, only to see Matthews fist it out to Billy
Minter, Woodward's successor at inside right, who knocked
it in. The final score was 3-0. After the near disaster at the
start of the game, the match had turned into a real holiday
treat for the crowd as the home team demonstrated its
undoubted superiority, with Woodward himself showing
some of his finest work.

By the turn of the year, Spurs were well on track for promotion at their first attempt. In fact they were doing better
in the Football League than they had done for a long time
in the Southern League: they had suffered fewer defeats in
the first half of the season than they had done for the last
seven years. But they needed to keep up the momentum. Of
course, one of the problems for Spurs in the New Year was
the perennial one of the Home International tournament
and Woodward's absence to play in those matches. Apart
from the way he pulled the forward line together, he was
also Spurs' leading goal-scorer, with eleven to his name.

For the time being, however, Spurs continued their fine
form. They took on and beat First Division Manchester City
4-2 away in the first round of the FA Cup. It could have been
more, but the referee, Mr Mason, seemed to have a strange
propensity to blow up for offside on a frequent basis. One
incident in particular was much criticised by the Tottenham
supporters who had made the trip to Manchester. This was
when Woodward passed the ball to Walton, who ran on and

kicked the ball into the net while the whistle was blowing. In fact, Walton had been behind Woodward when the pass was made. Nevertheless, 4-2 was a good score away at a First Division side and Woodward did more than enough to uphold his reputation in the North.

The next League match was again 'up North' and was a crucial encounter with promotion rivals Bolton. Once more, Woodward was on invincible form and he led his team to a 1-0 victory. Bolton's centre half, Greenhaigh, was no match for him and resorted to foul tactics, for which he was several times reprimanded by the referee. Fortunately, Woodward was not hurt in any of these encounters.

Woodward suffered again in his next match at home to Hull City. Hull had no answer to Woodward's clever runs through the centre and, in the second half, decided there was only one way to stop him and that wasn't the legal way! Woodward was kicked and pushed without much protection from the referee, who overlooked a number of clear fouls. One particular incident occurred when he was wilfully pushed in the back inside the penalty area. The crowd booed and jeered but the referee, Mr Bamlett, let it go. It is said that Woodward 'could not help casting a reproachful glance at the referee'. Woodward, of course, relied on the referee to deal with such incidents. He would not countenance retaliation of any sort, either by himself or his team-mates, so it was vital to him that the referee gave him his full protection and stopped the dubious tactics of his opponents. When this didn't happen, he naturally felt very aggrieved. In this match, Mr Bamlett did not inspire any confidence at all in the way he handled the game. The *Tottenham Herald* neatly summed up the feeling of the crowd at the way he had allowed their hero to be pushed, pulled and kicked, when it said, 'The spectators were in none too sweet a humour when the game finished, and if they had been confessors and Hull penitents, the penance would have been pretty severe.' The end result of all this was a 0-0 draw.

Reluctantly for Spurs, the time now came when they had to release their star to the international season. On 13 February, he captained the England side against Ireland, scoring two goals in a 4-0 victory. As it happened, his absence in the Tottenham team made little difference to the outcome of the League match played on the same day as they beat Blackpool 4-1, although, even then, *the Tottenham Herald's* reporter gave his opinion that 'We expect there would have been a wider margin between the scores if Vivian Woodward had been playing. MacFarlane, who took his place, performed with a very fair degree of skill, but it seemed that the other inside forwards showed a certain want of confidence in him, as they did not pass to him so readily as they would do to Woodward, and indulged in more dribbling than usual.'

If it wasn't bad enough that Spurs were losing Woodward for the Home Internationals, on 27 February he was chosen for the Football League in an encounter with the Scottish League. He scored his side's only goal in a 3-1 defeat. The Scots were not too impressed with his play and Scottish papers found him 'not sufficiently robust' to deal with their defenders. Of course this was a constant theme throughout Woodward's career, going right back to the days when his father did not want him to play football at all. But what he lacked in physique and strength, he had always made up for in fast, intelligent play. His shots were hardly ever particularly fierce shots, but he scored his high number of goals through clever placement and by fooling the goalkeeper.

Cigarette cards were also becoming popular and Woodward
featured on those too. Above left is a card from the
Taddy & Co. series 'Prominent Footballers', produced in
1907. Above right is a more modern card from a series called
England's Top Goalscorers, drawn by Phil Neill (which includes
Gary Lineker, Alan Shearer and Bobby Charlton amongst others)
just to show he has not been forgotten.

Spurs first home League defeat came on 13 March to
West Bromwich Albion. 35,000 spectators saw the match
which led to Spurs being deposed from the number one
spot in the table by the team which beat them. The Spurs
forward line was not its usual commanding self and, although
Woodward distributed the ball well, the other forwards
wasted chance after chance. The final score was 1-3.

Two days later Woodward was back on international
duty for England against Wales. The final score was 2-0 in
England's favour, but Woodward did not score.

Following the match against West Bromwich Albion, it seemed that they (West Brom) had the League sewn up, leaving Spurs and Bolton to battle it out for the one remaining promotion place. Tottenham's next League encounter was away at Birmingham. It was vital they did not lose, and, although the general opinion was that they had had the best of the game, with just a few minutes of the match remaining, they were 3-2 down. Woodward had played another brilliant game, but he was matched by the Birmingham goalkeeper, Dorrington – but for whom, Spurs would surely have won by two or three goals. However, in the dying seconds, the Spurs inside left, Bob Steel, dribbled the ball through and passed to Woodward, who finally managed to get it past Dorrington, making the score 3-3 and thereby saving a crucial point.

There was a strange start to Tottenham's next home match as the kick-off was delayed until 4.00 p.m. to allow time for Woodward to get to White Hart Lane. He had been best man at a wedding earlier in the day. A rumour went round the ground that it was Woodward himself who had been married and that he had chosen to start his honeymoon by participating in that afternoon's match against Gainsborough. However, this was not the case. In the event, it was just as well for Spurs that they did delay the start and that he did play, because the other forwards did not have a good day. Woodward brought what cohesion there was into their attacks and whenever there was a dangerous attack, he was involved in it somewhere. Unfortunately he received a nasty blow on the ankle in the first half, and seemed to feel the effects for the rest of the game, though, even so, he still stood out head and shoulders above his colleagues. The one goal scored by Spurs was, of course, by Woodward, but this was equalled by Gainsborough. It was a point dropped by Tottenham, and one they could ill afford to lose.

The ankle injury kept him out of the final international of the season against Scotland and the following League match, against Grimsby, but he was able to return for the 9 April League match against Clapton Orient, although he was still not fully fit with the result that he was unable to give of his best and another 2 points were wasted as Clapton Orient won 1-0.

With Bolton pushing hard for second spot, Spurs needed an away victory at Turf Moor on 17 April if they were going to remain in the driving seat. This was not going to be an easy match, as it was Burnley who had knocked them out of the FA Cup earlier in the season. Fortunately, Woodward was back to his best form and opened the scoring with a clever header and then added another before half-time. The final score was Burnley 1 Spurs 2. It was a vital win as it kept Tottenham in second place on goal average by just 1/31 of a goal and, once again, it was essentially down to Woodward's brilliance as it was his two goals that Spurs had to thank for their victory.

Fellow League debutants, Bradford Park Avenue, were the opposition for the next match, in which – in spite of being badly hurt following a particularly nasty foul – Woodward contributed one of the three goals in the 3-1 win. At least a draw from their final match of the season away to Derby was needed to ensure promotion. At half-time the score was Derby 1 Tottenham 0, but a goal from Bob Steel in the second half gave them the point they needed. It was not a great game, but Spurs had done it. Promoted to football's First Division after just one season.

The team's homecoming from Derby revived memories of their return following the FA Cup win back in 1901. On their arrival at St Pancras station they found it filled with crowds of cheering spectators. There were thousands of supporters present both inside and outside the station. As the made their way back to Tottenham they were joined by a band at Seven Sisters. A reception was held at the Tottenham Palace, where speeches were made and the health of the team drunk. All Tottenham seemed to be out on the streets that night and the festivities did not finish until 3.00 a.m. the following morning. In two seasons, Spurs had gone from the Southern League to the First Division. Much of this was undoubtedly due to Woodward's inspirational play and leadership. Although it could not be said that he had single-handedly been responsible for their rapid rise, it must remain very doubtful whether Spurs would have managed their wonderful achievement without him. His contribution was recognised by the Football League itself as he was named their Player of the Year.

Following the end of the season, Tottenham went off on a tour of Argentina and Uruguay, but Woodward did not go with them. Instead he went on a mini-tour of Europe as captain of the England amateur team, beating Switzerland 9-0 in Basle on 20 May and France 11-0 in Paris on 22 May. Apart from his leadership, Woodward contributed four goals to the win over Switzerland and one to the victory over France.

On his return to Britain, and less than one month after Spurs' triumphal end to the season, Vivian Woodward announced his intention to retire from top class football, citing the demands of his architectural practice as the reason.

THE SPENCER CRICKET & LAWN TENNIS CLUB (1901-1914)

On his full-time removal to London, Woodward decided to further his cricket career by joining one of London's top clubs of the period, the Spencer Cricket & Lawn Tennis Club. The cricket club had been founded in 1872 and played their first matches on Wandsworth Common on ground allocated to them by Lord Spencer, the lord of the manor. The club was named in his honour. The club moved to its own ground the following year and, in 1880, a lawn tennis club was added.

By the turn of the century the Spencer Cricket Club had begun to attract many of the leading club players of the time and had become one of the strongest in London. In 1901 they were planning to move yet again to a ground in Lyford Road and it was in this year that Vivian Woodward joined both clubs – on top of his football and cricket exploits he was no mean tennis player as well.

The move was finally completed in 1903, and in 1904 Woodward was appointed vice-captain of the cricket club. Of fifteen matches played that year, the Spencer Cricket Club won twelve. More success followed the following year, when, out of 23 matches, only 2 were lost. One of Woodward's colleagues at this time was the Surrey spin bowler, E.C. Kirk, which gives some indication of the team's strength.

In 1907, Woodward was appointed club captain. A short history of the club published in 1921 had this to say about him, 'V.J. Woodward took over the cricket captaincy, and the Club was most fortunate in securing such a personi-fication of sport in the very best sense of the word, and during his tenure of office the standard of cricket was even better than under the late skipper, H.W. Wheeler.' Once again it seems his sportsmanship and leadership were recognised.

The following season, Woodward topped the team's batting averages, and, as if that wasn't enough, he also won the Spencer Club Lawn Tennis Championship. Woodward's non-football expertise at sport didn't stop there, as he found time to take part in the new Edwardian craze of roller-skating and he was often to be found at the Olympia rink trying to improve his prowess. He was also a dab hand on the billiards table.

Although he was not Spencer's first choice as wicket-keeper, Woodward substituted on those occasions when the first team 'keeper was absent. He developed a particularly good relationship with Kirk and the two of them not infrequently contrived to get the opposition batsmen stumped. As captain he not only led his team expertly and with unsurpassed judgment on the field, but also made himself responsible for organising the social side of the club. In fact, during the summer months he gave up nearly all his spare time for the club, to which he was devoted – even to the extent of missing the start of the football season with Spurs to turn out for the cricket club and to represent the tennis club in the Essex Lawn Tennis Championships. It was all part of his philosophy that sport should be fun and not be taken too seriously.

Woodward continued as captain until 1910, in which year he was unable to play cricket during the summer owing to the England football tour of South Africa. He returned to the side in 1911, though not as captain. Although absent for the whole of the 1910 season and not playing any cricket for nearly two years, Woodward showed that he had lost none of his skill as he once again topped the side's batting averages with 1,067 runs scored at an average of 62.7. Of the 31 matches played that year, 20 were won, 7 drawn and only 4 lost.

It was a similar story in 1912 as the team lost just four matches out of 29 played, with Woodward yet again in good form with the bat. Once again he reached the final of the Lawn Tennis Championship, this time losing to F.F. Boles. It was a similar story in 1913, even to the extent of Woodward once again losing in the Lawn Tennis final to F.F. Boles again.

When the 1914 season opened, Woodward was again outstanding, but before the season was over the First World War had been declared and many players, including Woodward himself, had enlisted for the Army and were no longer available to play cricket for the club.

He did not return after the war.

1. A studio portrait of the great man.

2. Vivian's father, John Woodward.

3. Vivian's school, Ascham College, Clacton-on-Sea. This has been demolished and replaced by the town's telephone exchange.

4. *Right:* Woodward at the age of twenty-one. This photograph appeared in the 8 December 1900 edition of the *Clacton Graphic.* The original caption read, 'Clacton's centre forward, and whose play for the county, in the match Essex *v.* Suffolk at Colchester, last Thursday week, was so favourably commented on by the newspapers'.

5. *Below:* Clacton Town Football Club 1899/1900: the year they did the double. From left to right, back row (players only): Starling, Harding, Thompson, Stroud. Middle row: Pudney, McKinnon, Woodward, Roberts, Rattee, Duval. Front row: Mathams.

6. The Chelmsford team that won the Essex Senior Cup, 1901/02. Woodward is sitting second from the left in the front row.

7. The legendary C.B. Fry who predicted that Woodward 'may become a great player'.

The Stadium, Franco-British Exhibition, London, 1908

8. The White City Stadium, London, where the 1908 Olympic Games football tournament was held.

9. The United Kingdom gold medal-winning team at the 1908 Olympics. Woodward is in the centre of the front row.

10. The England team which toured Austria–Hungary in 1908. From left to right, back row: Hardy, Greenhaigh, Bridgett, Warren, Lintott, Lewis, Compton, Pennington, Bradshaw, Rutherford. Front row: Wedlock, Windridge, Woodward, Hilsdon.

11. The 1908/09 Tottenham Hotspur team. This was their first full season in the Football League. From left to right, back row: T. Deacock (director), Walton, Morris, Minter, Hewitson, Burton, Coquet, M. Cadman (director), Nie (trainer). Front row: R. Steele, Woodward, D. Steele, Middlemiss, Darnell.

12. The England team which toured South Africa in 1910. From left to right, back row: Benson, Duckworth, Leeming, Hayes, Wall. Middle row: F. Hughes (honorary manager), Silto, Wright, Raine, Bulcock, Richards, Sturgess, Yeadon (trainer). Front row: Berry, Fleming, Hibbert, Wedlock, C. Hughes (manager), Woodward, Lievesley, Holley, Sharpe.

VIVIAN J. WOODWARD.
Tottenham Hotspur F.C. and England's Centre Forward, 1903-4.
Published by Walter Henry, 11, Prince's Street Westminster, S.W.　Copyright.

Nov. 1906
Vivian J. Woodward. Tottenham Hotspurs

13-16. The height of Woodward's fame coincided with the Edwardian postcard boom. These are four postcards produced of him during that period. No. 13 (above) dates from 1903/04, No. 14 (left) from 1906, No. 15 (opposite above) from 1908/09 and No. 16 (opposite below) is undated. All these postcards show clearly Woodward's taste in shorts. A Clacton colleague of his, Freddie Baxfield, once said, 'With his hands in his pockets, and his three-quarter length shorts, he looked more like the referee than a player, but once he had the ball he showed you that he WAS a player all right… When he went on the field he inspired you with confidence.'

Vivian. J. Woodward
Tottenham Hotspur
1908-1909.

Vivian Woodward

17. Chelsea Football Club for the 1910/11 season. From left to right, back row: Moir (assistant trainer), McConnel, Jones, Douglas, Molyneux, Dolby, McRoberts, Taylor, Cousins, Walton, Woodward. Second row: Harding, Whittingham, Hilsdon, A. Wileman, Horn, Whitley, Bowles, H. Wileman, Cane, Clark (head groundsman), Ranson (trainer), Calderhead Jr. Third row: Calderhead (secretary-manager), Schomberg, Boyer, Kinton, Maltby (all directors), Kirby (chairman), H. Mears, J. Mears, Parker (all directors), J. Palmer (reserve team manager), A. Palmer (assistant secretary). Front row: Fairgray, Ormiston, Freeman, Downing, Windridge (captain), Cartwright, McEwan, Cameron, Brawn, Bettridge, McKenzie.

18. The opening ceremony for the 1912 Olympic Games in Stockholm. Woodward had the honour of carrying the British flag

19. A scene from the 1912 Olympic Games semi-final between Great Britain (in white) and Finland.

20. The 1912 Olympic final between Great Britain and Denmark in progress.

21. The Great Britain gold medal–winning team at the 1912 Olympics. Woodward is in the centre of the front row.

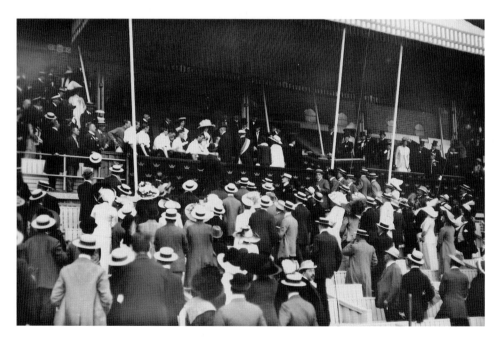

22. Vivian Woodward receiving the 1912 Olympic gold medal from King Gustav of Sweden.

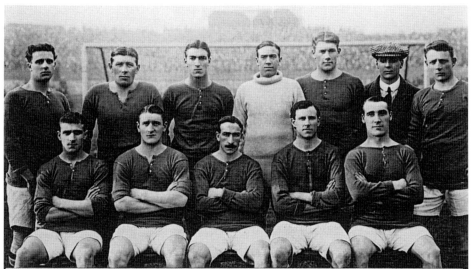

The First CHELSEA Team To Beat ASTON VILLA, Oct 25th 1913.

23. *Above:* A photograph taken at Villa Park on 25 October 1913 of the Chelsea team which beat Aston Villa – the first time they had achieved this feat. Woodward, who played at inside left, is second from the right in the front row.

24. *Right:* The Spencer Cricket & Lawn Tennis Club's roll of honour commemorating its members who fought in the First World War. Vivian Woodward's name is one from the end.

CHELSEA v MANCHESTER UNITED

FOOTBALL LEAGUE MATCH

Monday, April 19th, 1915   *Kick-off 5.30 p.m.*

CHELSEA (Blue)

1
MOLYNEUX
Goal

2   3
BETTRIDGE   **SHARP**
Right Back   Left Back

4   5   6
TAYLOR   **LOGAN**   **ABRAMS**
Right Half   Centre Half   Left Half

7   8   9   10   11
FORD **V. J. WOODWARD** **BRITTAN** **CROAL** **McNEIL**
Outside Right Inside Right Centre Inside Left Outside Left

12   13   14   15   16
WALL **WEST** **ANDERSON** **POTTS** **MEREDITH**
Outside Left Inside Left Centre Inside Right Outside Right

17   18   19
HAYWOOD **O'CONNELL** **MONTGOMERY**
Left Half Centre Half Right Half

20   21
SPRATT   **HODGE**
Left Back   Right Back

22
BEALE
Goal

MANCHESTER UNITED (Red)

Referee - - - Mr. C. ILLSLEY (Smethwick).

Linesmen - - - Messrs. F. A. CLARKE and E. E. SMALL.

ANY ALTERATIONS WILL BE NOTIFIED ON THE BOARD

Printed and Published for the Proprietors (The Chelsea Football and Athletic Co., Ltd.), by Jas. Truscott & Son, Ltd., London.

25. Woodward's last Football League match was for Chelsea against Manchester United on 19 April 1915.

1.—Gilling calling for cheers for the losers.

2.—V. J. Woodward and A. Gilling (captain)

3.—Gilling receiving the cup from Mr. A. Crowther (Vice-President of the County Association

4.—The Clacton Team and some of the Officials.

Photos : J. E. Stutter, Colchester.

26. *Above:* A photographic tribute to Clacton Town FC which appeared in the 1 May 1920 edition of the *Clacton Graphic* to commemorate their victory in the Pearson Cup final. Left: Clacton's captain Adrian Gilling calls for cheers for the losers. Top: Woodward and Gilling with the cup. Right: Gilling receiving the cup from Mr Crowther. Bottom: The victorious Clacton team.

27. *Right:* A photograph showing Woodward's dominance in the air.

Vivian Woodward, Great Amateur, Dies Aged 74

By J. G. ORANGE

VIVIAN J. WOODWARD, one of the greatest centre-forwards England ever had, died last night, aged 74, at a nursing home at Ealing. He had been ill for four years.

Woodward had a most illustrious career. He was a director of Tottenham Hotspur as well as

Vivian Woodward—an early picture taken in his international days.

their centre-forward. He was also a director of Chelsea during the time he played for that club.

For many years he was England's centre-forward or inside-right and, including his amateur and Olympic Games honours, played for England more often than any other player.

He was an out-and out amateur. Directors of the Spurs and Chelsea have told me they could not get him to charge his bus fares for matches

He played entirely for his love of the game, and under a code which nowadays would be thought not to belong to this world

28. The *Evening News* obituary to Vivian Woodward.

THREE

CHELSEA
(1909-1919)

Following his retirement from League football, Woodward returned to Chelmsford for the 1909/10 season. This was well underway by the time of his first outing on 12 October 1909 away to Barking in the South Essex League. 1,300 spectators turned out to watch the international's return. Although he hadn't played for several months and was making a late return because of his business commitments, it was soon evident that he had lost none of his ball control skill and his passing ability was as accurate as ever. It was not a happy return in the sense that Barking won 3-2, but, in all other respects, it was most satisfactory.

The following week he gave even more evidence that his expertise was as consummate as ever as he banged in five for Chelmsford in the 6-2 victory over the 3rd Grenadier Guards. A few days later, Woodward was chosen to captain the England team in an amateur international against Sweden. England's 7-0 victory owed much to Woodward's generalship as the forward line proved to be much too fast and clever for the Swedes, and, although Woodward only scored one goal himself, he was instrumental in making the rest. He was immediately chosen to captain the side again against Ireland on 20 November. Following that match, in which he scored yet another clever goal, Woodward stunned the football world by announcing his return to the big time, though not to Tottenham.

Chelsea had been going through a very bad patch and were heading towards the bottom of the First Division at an alarming rate. Seven of their first team players were injured, including the whole of their first choice forward line, and a very inept performance at home to Bradford City on 20 November, which they lost 3–0, convinced the Chelsea directors that something drastic was needed to save them from relegation. More in hope than confidence they approached Woodward and much to their surprise – and everyone else's – he agreed to return to help them out till the end of the season in view of their circumstances.

The *Chelsea FC Chronicle* (Chelsea's official matchday programme) was ecstatic, 'We have had so much bad luck of late that, when a genuine piece of the right stuff comes along, we may be pardoned for sitting down and making a proper meal of it. The Bradford result was about the climax of trouble and, we had just got out our miserable looks and our "humpy" speeches when suddenly something occurred to lift us out of the doldrums. There was many a glad smile round the regions of Stamford Bridge when it was announced that Vivian J. Woodward had thrown in his lot with the Chelsea Club.

Possibly Chelsea never have had such a slice of luck. I should say that without a doubt Vivian Woodward is the most popular man in football today. Popular with players, popular with the spectators wherever and whenever he plays, he owes his unique position chiefly to one thing. First, foremost, and all the time he is a gentleman. He may play well or he may play moderately (he never plays badly), but no matter how he plays his very presence in a team is ever a great factor of success. He inspires his men with his unflagging energy. He inspires a confidence in them as no other player could ever do. I do not think that there is any doubt that Vivian Woodward was mainly responsible for Tottenham Hotspur's sensational rise to the First Division.'

Unable to believe its luck, Chelsea, via The *Chronicle*, returned to the theme the following week: 'The most cheering news we have had during our time of desolation is the intimation that Vivian John Woodward is going to assist Chelsea. Had the great Vivian been a professional player his transfer fee, I fancy, would have been something near a record one. Instead Woodward comes to us for love, and we may take it that he is already the idol of Stamford Bridge. Vivian Woodward always has been and ever will be the people's favourite. Small wonder. Great as he is as a player, his first claim to popularity lies in the fact that he has ever been first and foremost a gentleman. I question if any footballer has ever been so universally popular, and he carries his honours with the air of a bashful *debutant*. Honours have been showered upon him, and never has he been known, either on or off the field, to belie his title of the perfect gentleman.'

To many football followers of the time it was not clear why Woodward, having given up top-class football with Tottenham after seeing them rise from a Southern League club to a First Division team, should then return less than six months later to Chelsea. At the time of his retirement he said he was unable to reconcile the needs of football with the needs of his architectural business. There were

This cartoon appeared in the 4 December 1909 issue of the *Chelsea Chronicle*. It neatly sums up the hopes they placed in Woodward to save them from relegation.

dark mutterings about a falling-out between Woodward and Spurs and that that was the real reason why he had left them. Woodward himself denied this, saying that he and the Spurs directors had always been, and still remained, the best of friends and he hoped this would continue in the future in spite of his decision to move to Chelsea. In an interview with *The Athletic News*, he said the reason for his move was because Chelsea at the present time was in the most unfortunate position of having practically a senior forward line on the injured list. He went on to say, 'Mr Kirby, the chairman of Chelsea, wrote to me a few days ago pointing this out, and explained how difficult his club found it to complete a side, especially in attack. He reminded me in his letter that three seasons ago, I promised that if ever I was a freelance I would come to Chelsea if they thought I could be of any service to them. When I received Mr Kirby's letter I immediately recalled my promise. I replied that if a place was found for me, I would endeavour to do my best to fill it.' He added that another reason which had swayed his decision was that a number of his relatives and friends, all keenly interested in football, lived in the Chelsea district and that Stamford Bridge was much nearer his own home than White Hart Lane.

For Woodward, true to his nature, it was nothing more nor less than honouring a promise he had made three years previously. In addition to that it is probably the case that his business commitments had lessened quicker than he thought. Certainly he had returned to football with Chelmsford and had already captained his country in two amateur internationals. There is no doubt he was certainly touched by Chelsea's plight and the fact they had seven of their first team injured – including the whole of their forward line. Initially his return was to be only until the end of the season. Much now rested on his shoulders and he had taken a lot on as the Stamford Bridge faithful were expecting him, almost single-handedly, to keep them out of the relegation zone and to ensure their place in the

First Division. Woodward, of course, was used to these high expectations and there was certainly a confidence about him that would have led him to feel that he could do it for his new team.

It must surely also have been the case that Woodward missed football at the highest level. He may have been a good architect, but it was in the football world that he really excelled and where he was at home. Perhaps he had discovered that, in spite of being an amateur, football was in fact his business, not architecture. And while playing for Chelmsford may have satisfied his need to play football *per se*, he would certainly have felt that he needed the competitive edge that only top-class football could give him and that he was not being extended.

Woodward's debut for Chelsea was pencilled in for 27 November 1909 away at Sheffield Wednesday in a First Division match. It is a strange fact that, after over six years as an England international, including several years as captain, he was about to play, for the first time in his life, in First Division football. It was to prove to be an unhappy first outing for Woodward as his new team were badly beaten 4-1. It was their seventh loss in eight games. It was obvious that retaining First Division status was going to be an uphill struggle for the Pensioners, Woodward or no Woodward.

However, Chelsea did not have to wait long for the much-hoped-for Woodward-inspired improvement. On his home debut at Stamford Bridge the following week, on 4 December, he helped them to a 4-1 victory over Bristol City. As well as scoring two of the goals from headers, he managed to get the forward line working as a team. In particular, as inside right, he gave the outside right, Billy

Brawn, more chances to use the ball than he had had all season and he took full advantage of it. As a pair on the right wing, Woodward and Brawn took the Bristol defence apart. With this win, Chelsea moved from second from bottom to fifth from bottom. Already Woodward had restored hope.

Unfortunately for Chelsea, but extremely fortunately for England as it turned out, Woodward missed the Pensioners' next game as he was playing another amateur international, this time against Holland at Stamford Bridge. It was to be one of the most remarkable performances of his career as he captained the England amateur team to a 9-1 victory over The Netherlands – a feat made all the more outstanding given the fact that for over an hour of the match, England had just ten players. Woodward organised his forwards to give one of the best displays ever seen on an international field as he decided that the way to beat Holland was to outpace them with a series of rapid short passing runs. The Dutch defence worked hard but they just could not cope with this tactic. Once again it was a matter of Woodward using his brain rather than just brute force. His own personal reward in all of this was to score six of the goals himself. It was a dazzling display and proved, if further proof were needed, that he was still at the very peak of his form.

Without their star player, however, Chelsea went down to another defeat, losing this time 4-2 at Bury. Woodward was also absent from their next game at home to Tottenham. It was felt that this may have been a diplomatic absence! He also missed the Christmas Day fixture against Notts County, as he was, as usual, visiting his relatives in Clacton.

He was back for the Boxing Day meeting at Stamford Bridge against the current First Division Champions, Newcastle. In front of a record crowd, Chelsea played

their best game of the season as they overcame a tough
Newcastle side 2-1. And this was in spite of the fact that
they were down to ten men for most of the match as their
centre half, Edward Birnie, was injured in the first half and
taken off, to be replaced by the centre forward, Evan Jones,
leaving the forward line with just four men.

With the score 1-1 at half-time things looked ominous
for the Pensioners, but they held their nerve and, with just
20 minutes to go, the ball fell at Woodward's feet. He made
a quick pass out to Brawn on the right wing who made
a high cross back to the goal mouth where Woodward's
head met it perfectly, guiding it into the net. The cheering that greeted this perfectly worked goal lasted for several minutes. This was the only goal to be scored in the
second half, leaving the final score Chelsea 2 Newcastle 1.
Unfortunately, although they played well in the New Year
return match, the Chelsea forwards could not repeat the
trick and the team went down 1-0.

Worse was to follow as they were thumped 5-1 by
Liverpool at Anfield, Woodward scoring Chelsea's solitary
goal. An FA Cup win over Hull City was followed by
another disappointing League result, this time a 0-0 draw
at home to Aston Villa. Worse was to come on 12 February
1910 as they lost 5-2 away to Bolton. Woodward missed this
match as he was once again on amateur international duty
in Belfast. Chelsea were in dire trouble as they dropped
back to two from bottom. Relief came on 19 February as
they beat Middlesbrough 2-1 at home. It was Chelsea's first
League victory since Boxing Day and achieved without
Woodward, who had a slight injury.

The next match looked to be a tough one for the
struggling Pensioners as they were up against third-placed

Blackburn Rovers. But with Woodward back in the side, it actually proved relatively easy as he stamped his authority on the game, leading his side to a 3-1 victory, scoring the third goal himself.

The next match, away at Nottingham Forest, ended in a 0-0 draw but a controversial incident in the second half completely overshadowed the game. Chelsea's inside left Jimmie Windridge had been provoked by Notts Forest's Needham all match and decided he couldn't take any more of it. A fight broke out between the two, witnessed by the linesman, who flagged the referee, Mr Briggs, who called a halt to play. After two minutes of discussion between the two, Mr Briggs sent both players off. Chelsea had already lost one player through injury in the first half and so were now down to nine men. That they held on to draw the match was a creditable feat. At the end of play the police came onto the field and escorted the referee off through hoards of angry spectators from both sides.

Following a 4-0 defeat at home to Sunderland and a 0-0 draw with Everton, things were not looking good for Chelsea. To add to their problems, Woodward missed a number of matches through injury and did not return until 29 April for the penultimate League match and last home game, against Bury, by which time Chelsea were one from bottom and staring into the abyss. The local paper, the *Chelsea Mail*, was pleased to report that 'The return of Woodward brought a marked improvement in the attack... from the start Chelsea showed better football.' The final result was 2-0 to Chelsea and a last lifeline to escape relegation as their final match of the season was, ironically, away to Spurs, who, as fate would have it, were their rivals for the second relegation spot,

Bolton having already been relegated. Whoever won the match would stay up. Unfortunately it was not to be for Chelsea as they lost the match. Chelsea were down and Spurs stayed up.

In spite of their drop into the Second Division, Chelsea remained optimistic about the future and at the start of the next season the *Chelsea Chronicle*'s opinion was that 'if we can but steer clear of accidents we have a team which should carry us back into the First Division... we doubt if any club in the country has a better forward line.' Although Woodward returned from South Africa later than the rest of the team and was, in consequence, late for the start of the season, he nevertheless agreed to continue playing for Chelsea and made his first appearance in an FA Cup tie against Clapton at Stamford Bridge on 19 September and his first League appearance came the following week against Wolverhampton Wanderers.

Although when he signed for Chelsea the previous season he had intimated that it was only to help them over a bad patch, his signal success on the South African tour had convinced him that he should continue to play in top-class football and so he agreed to sign amateur forms for the Pensioners for the 1910/11 season. Once again Chelsea's gain was Chelmsford's loss.

For the first few matches of the new season, Woodward played at the unaccustomed position of inside left, but it didn't seem to make much difference to his command of the field or his authority over the team. The match against Lincoln City on 4 November was the highlight of his and Chelsea's early season form as he scored two and made the rest in a 7-0 demolition.

On 25 November Chelsea travelled to the Hawthorns to meet top-of-the-table West Bromwich Albion. It was Chelsea, however, who came out on top. Woodward opened the scoring for the visitors and they never looked back even though, once again, Woodward's skill was answered by some rather rough play in the second half. Chelsea ran out 3-1 winners to put themselves well on course for promotion.

However, with one win, one draw and one loss in December, Chelsea needed some good results from their Christmas programme if they were stay in with a chance of going up. This year saw no exception to Woodward's determination to spend at least part of Christmas with his family and he missed the Boxing Day game against Leeds, although he did turn out in both the Christmas Eve and the day after Boxing Day games. It may be seen as significant that Chelsea won both the games he played in but could only draw the game he missed, though, in fairness to the rest of the team, it should be pointed out that the two he played in were at Stamford Bridge, while the other was away to Leeds at Elland Road.

It is interesting to note in passing that even though he had returned home to visit his sister, he still couldn't quite keep away from football and, on Boxing Day, he found himself an interested spectator at the friendly match played between his old club, Clacton Town, and Brightlingsea.

The last match of the year on the last day of the year saw Woodward up against his leading rival as England's top goalscorer when Steve Bloomer's Derby County paid a visit to Stamford Bridge. In spite of a 3-2 win for Chelsea, it was not a happy occasion for either Woodward or Chelsea as he was injured early on in the match. Although a passenger for much of the first half he stayed on the pitch, moving to outside left. He sustained a further injury in the second half and went off, and though he pluckily returned a few minutes later, he could only limp along the touchline until the final whistle came.

This injury put Woodward out of the team for the next six matches and he did not return until the FA Cup second round encounter away at Chesterfield Town on 4 February. And what a return! Two goals and a 4-1 victory to put Chelsea into the third round. In spite of his magnificent resumption of football, Woodward missed the next two League matches but was back again for the next FA Cup match, away at Wolverhampton Wanderers. This time Woodward was back to his favoured position of inside right. Yet again he made a splendid Cup return and after just 15 minutes had the ball in the back of the net with a low, well-placed shot from the edge of the eighteen-yard box following some excellent combination play by the forwards. It was a brilliant Cup victory as Chelsea ran out 2-0 winners.

A combination of wishing to make sure his injury had healed sufficiently, his business commitments and international matches kept Woodward out of the side for several more fixtures and it was once again the importance of the FA Cup, this time the semi-final, which brought him back into the team, Chelsea having won the quarter-final match at home to Swindon without him.

The reason for missing the quarter-final match was his last appearance in a full international as he played at inside left against Wales. In spite of his ups and downs that season, playing for his country seemed to bring out the best in him again as he put two goals past Robert Evans, the Welsh goalkeeper, in England's 3-0 win. Altogether Woodward had appeared in 23 full internationals (13 as captain) and scored 29 goals. Earlier, he had also captained the England amateur international side against Wales, winning 5-1.

Unfortunately, Woodward was badly injured during the FA Cup semi-final against Newcastle, breaking a small bone in his arm. It affected his play in the match itself, with the result that Chelsea failed to reach the final, losing 3-0 to the powerful Newcastle team. Following the disappointment of going out of the Cup at the last hurdle, Chelsea put all their efforts into winning promotion. It was unfortunate that Woodward's injury prevented him from returning to the Chelsea team on a regular basis at this crucial time. Of the next six games, he only managed to turn out in one. This was on 14 April – a home encounter with Leeds United – which Chelsea won 4-1, Woodward scoring a goal.

With three matches to go, Chelsea needed four points (at that time it was two points for a win) to be sure of promotion. The first was a home match to Burnley on 22 April. Woodward resumed his place at inside right. All the Chelsea forwards had a fine match and peppered the Burnley goal, but some fine saves by Dawson, the Burnley goalkeeper, kept the score at 0-0 as they went in for half-time. It was the same story at the start of the second half. A shot from Woodward just grazed the post and then a header, that looked for all the world as if it was going in, was miraculously saved by Dawson. At last the breakthrough came as Woodward managed to get a rather scrappy goal. Two more quickly followed and Chelsea had gained their first objective, winning 3-0.

With just two more points needed, Chelsea found themselves playing away in the last two matches. The first of these was against their rivals for promotion, Bolton (West Bromwich Albion having already secured the first spot). It was not a brilliant match from Chelsea's point of view. They seemed to lack the fire and spirit of Bolton. It's an old sporting cliché that results in important matches depend on who wants the victory most. In this case it most certainly seemed that Bolton wanted it more. Still in the process of recovering from injury, Woodward gave a somewhat lacklustre performance and was unable either to marshal his troops well or shoot accurately when given the opportunity. The net result of all this was that Bolton won 2-0.

Although losing to Bolton had been a severe blow, Chelsea still had one last chance. If they could beat Gainsborough Trinity, who were just one from bottom in the table, in the last match of the season they would still get second place and therefore promotion on goal average. But it was not to be. In spite of a better performance by Woodward, which included his side's only goal, Gainsborough took the match 3-1. Chelsea had to be content with third place and another season in the Second Division.

It had not been a good season for Woodward. The injury sustained in the match on 31 December against Derby had not only put him out for a number of games – he only played in 19 out of 38 League matches – but also seemed to affect his play when he did return. During 1911, he certainly was not the world class footballer that everyone had come to expect and, for the first time in his life, he actually turned in a couple of poor performances. As this would be the first summer since 1907 that he had no summer tours to undertake, both Woodward and Chelsea could only hope that a good rest from football during the close season would help him recover his form.

He returned to the Chelsea line-up for their fifth match of the 1911/12 season against Wolves. Much to the relief of everyone, the local paper was able to report that Chelsea's 4-0 victory was 'achieved by some sparkling play among the inside forwards, Freeman, Woodward and, in a lesser degree, by Brown.' Woodward scored the fourth goal with a first-time drive having already been instrumental in passes leading to the other goals. It looked as though the summer rest from football had had its effect and that V.J. Woodward was back to his best!

Woodward played in the next four matches, swapping between inside right and centre forward. On 21 October he led England's amateur international team to a 3-0 victory over Denmark.

Woodward was now playing less and less a part in Chelsea's plans. Once again his business commitments were preventing him from appearing regularly, though he did answer his country's call when required, as, for example, on 19 November when he captained the England amateur side against Ireland at Huddersfield, scoring one goal in England's 2-0 victory. Woodward did not return to Chelsea's first team until 2 December, when he played in the unaccustomed role of inside left against Glossop North End. He played again on 9 December at inside left, against Hull City, then did not appear again for Chelsea until 2 March 1912.

In the meantime, he had returned to his roots, putting in a surprise appearance for Clacton Town in their Pearson Cup match away to Harwich & Parkeston. As word of his playing spread the crowd grew and grew until more than a thousand people were inside Harwich's Royal Oak ground. For those not at the match and hearing the result later it must have been a big surprise to learn that Clacton had beaten Harwich 2-1, but for those who knew that Woodward was playing perhaps the only surprise was that the score line was not bigger. Woodward scored both the Clacton goals.

The following week, he took his place in the Clacton Town line-up in a home match against Colchester Town (attracting the biggest gate of the season at their Old Road ground). As in the previous week, he unselfishly sought to bring his colleagues into play by distributing the ball around rather than try to dribble through by himself, which, in this class of play, he could undoubtedly have done. The final score this time was 2-2, with Woodward heading in a beautifully placed goal.

Woodward's next match for Clacton was the Boxing Day friendly against Page Green Old Boys, while his next 'serious' match was away at Hoffman's Athletic in the North Essex League. Once again, a large crowd turned out at Hoffman's ground in Chelmsford to see the former Chelmsford player. By now, the Clacton players were getting more used to Woodward's method of play and his passing technique and were able to take more advantage of it, with the result that they ran out 7-2 victors, Woodward himself scoring a great hat-trick.

Woodward's appearance in Clacton's colours had prompted the *Daily Express* to send a reporter to the match. Their comment was that 'In spite of the heavy going, he exhibited all his old-time cleverness, his footwork being as brilliant as ever. Besides obtaining three goals, he was mainly responsible for the other four.'

He turned out for Clacton for the last time this season on 21 January 1912 in a League match against Harwich & Parkeston. One particular piece of play just had the

Harwich team staring in amazement. Following some mid-field exchanges, Woodward gained possession of the ball with Challis, the opposing left-back, glued to his side. The international set off towards the goal, then ran across the goalmouth with Challis on the goal side of him. He then hooked the ball round Challis into the opposite corner of the net to which everyone expected. It was a marvellous piece of footwork and in a different class to anything seen on the Old Road ground for many years. The game resulted in yet another win for Clacton Town over Harwich & Parkeston, this time 2-1.

Altogether, Woodward turned out for his old club in five matches and had amazed the crowd (and the other players) in every one of them. He had received rapturous applause from the Clacton supporters and there were many wishing that if only he would give up the big time and come back to them...

Woodward's return to the Chelsea side came just as they were making their final push for promotion back to the First Division. He returned at inside left, but this time it was inside right, Bob Whittingham, who stole the show as he scored all three in the 3-0 victory over Clapton Orient.

Even though he had now reappeared in the team, Woodward did not turn out consistently and took part in only three of the next seven matches, although he did play in two more amateur internationals, captaining England to wins over Holland on 16 March and Belgium on 8 April, contributing one goal to the 4-0 victory over Holland and not scoring in the 2-1 defeat of Belgium.

With the run-in proving to be so important for Chelsea's chances of promotion, Woodward agreed to play in the last three matches. Although he did not score in any of them, he nevertheless played his usual pivotal role in securing victory in all three: 4–1 at home to Blackpool, 2–0 away at Barnsley and 1–0 at home to Bradford Park Avenue, with the result that Chelsea took second spot by two points over Burnley, ensuring promotion to the First Division.

Over the summer, Woodward captained the Great Britain football team in the 1912 Olympic Games (see chapter twelve). He returned after the cricket season to the Chelsea line-up for the fourth match on 14 September against Sheffield United – and it wasn't a moment too soon. Chelsea had endured a disastrous start to the season, losing all three of their opening matches. Back to his favoured inside right position, Woodward made all the difference to Chelsea as he inspired them to a 4–1 win, netting a hat-trick for himself.

Woodward continued to turn out for Chelsea on a much more regular basis than the previous season, though he did miss the match against Sunderland on 5 October as he was playing for England amateurs against Ireland amateurs in Belfast and again on 12 November as he was away scoring two goals in England amateurs' 4–0 victory over Belgium at Swindon.

In spite of Woodward's more regular presence, all was not well at Chelsea as they struggled in the top division. In general, Woodward was still outstanding in the forward line but his colleagues were unable to keep pace with him. A rare break in the gloom came on 30 November when, for once, the attack seemed to click and they managed to defeat Derby County 3–1, Bob Whittingham and William Bridgeman scoring one each with Woodward adding the finishing touch by deftly heading the ball from a finely placed centre from Harry Ford. But it was a false dawn and Chelsea continued to struggle, losing their next three home matches. The only light in the gloom was a creditable performance away at Sheffield United on 4 January 1913. After being 3-0 down, it looked for all the world as if another defeat was coming Chelsea's way. But a spirited performance by the Pensioners, led by Woodward, dragged the final score back to 3-3, Woodward himself scoring the third goal that gave them the draw.

Although Chelsea won their next match 5-2, it was an FA Cup match against Southend United and, in spite of the score, Southend put up a good performance – which only served to remind everyone of the paucity of Chelsea as a First Division side. Only Woodward earned the praise of reporters at the match as he scored a wonderful goal, dribbling half the length of the field before putting the final touch and guiding the ball into the net.

The second round of the Cup against Sheffield Wednesday seemed to underscore Chelsea's problems, as although Chelsea did manage to hold on for a draw originally, they were hammered 6-0 in the replay. Once again though, Woodward was singled out for mention in the papers, 'There were outstanding figures – and none more noteworthy than Vivian Woodward' was one typical example.

With relegation after just one season staring them in the face, Chelsea needed some reasonable results in their last few matches. It was at this point that Woodward was whisked off to captain the England amateur team again on another mini European tour over the Easter period. On 21 March he scored one goal in the 3-0 win over Germany in Berlin and then on 24 March he scored England's only goal in their 2-1 defeat by Holland in The Hague – the first time in 36 matches that the England amateur team had been beaten by a continental opponent.

For Chelsea this meant the loss of Woodward for the three Easter fixtures. Having lost the first two, the Pensioners were not looking forward to the Easter Monday fixture away at Liverpool, but, amazingly, and against all the odds, they managed to pull off a 2-1 victory. It gave Chelsea a lifeline and hope that they could yet avoid relegation. But the feeling of optimism didn't last long as in the very next match back home at Stamford Bridge, they were crushed 6-1 by Blackburn Rovers, Woodward salvaging a tiny bit of pride by scoring Chelsea's only goal.

The next two matches resulted in an away loss to Derby and a home win against Spurs. Fortunately for Chelsea, Notts County and Arsenal were having an even worse season than they were and the next match away to Middlesbrough at Ayresome Park was to prove the critical fixture. The game was a hardfought struggle, but at half-time Chelsea were in the lead by virtue of an own goal. Things were on a knife edge as Middlesbrough pressed hard, but after a break by the Chelsea forwards, they managed to win a corner kick, which found its way onto Woodward's head and into the back of the net. He had put the match beyond doubt and with it Chelsea's position in the First Division was secured.

In all Woodward had managed to make 30 League and Cup appearances this year, scoring 11 goals. It had been a struggle but he had played a large part in keeping Chelsea up.

Chelsea again started the 1913/14 season poorly and were without a win in their first three matches, including two games at home. Woodward returned in time for the fourth match at home to Manchester United, by which time the Chelsea manager, David Calderhead, decided it was time to make changes to the forward line. But in spite of this and Woodward's return, it was another home defeat. The local paper, the *Chelsea Mail*, in its last ever edition, reported that 'In an endeavour to strike a winning team the Chelsea management made considerable alterations in the forward line, but while Woodward, playing his first game of the season, was in excellent form, his colleagues altogether failed to play up to expectations.' It looked as though Chelsea were in for another rough season. The next match seemed to confirm this as they went down 6-1 to Burnley, Chelsea's only goal coming from a penalty.

However, with Woodward back in the forward line on a permanent basis, he was able to weave his magic and got the attack working together as only he knew how. Of the next five matches, Chelsea won four, including an away win at the previous year's runners-up, Aston Villa.

For the rest of 1913, Chelsea maintained an unbeaten record at Stamford Bridge, Woodward missing just one of those matches when he was on amateur international duty for England against The Netherlands at Hull on 15 November. England won 2-1, with Woodward contributing a goal.

Away from home, Chelsea were not doing so well and had to wait until 27 December before finding the winning touch in a match against Woodward's old club, Spurs, Woodward scoring one goal in the 2-1 victory. During this period, Woodward had been moving around the forward line and appeared as centre forward, inside right and inside left. He was no longer scoring prolifically, but was, as usual, the brains behind the team and the other members of the forward line looked to him to take the lead in all matters tactical.

Apart from beating Oldham Athletic 2-1 on 3 January, the start of 1914 was not as successful for Chelsea at Stamford Bridge as the end of 1913 had been. They lost three and drew one of their first four fixtures. Woodward missed the one drawn match, against Bolton on 10 February, as he was captaining the English amateur team against a representative Army side at Aldershot. This losing run was ended when they once again took on Tottenham, beating them 7-3 on 21 February. As it happened Woodward did not play in this match either as he was resting in advance of an amateur international match in Belgium on 24 February; a match which England won 8-1 with Woodward scoring.

In Woodward's next appearance for Chelsea, on 28 February, he played in the unaccustomed position of right half as his team went down 3-0 at home to Aston Villa. He soon reverted to a more accustomed position as he turned out at centre forward for the next match against Middlesbrough.

From March onwards, the Chelsea team returned to the winning at home, losing away habit that they had shown earlier. By now, much interest had gone out of the season in the sense that they were comfortably mid-table: no chance of glory, but equally no danger of relegation. In the end Chelsea finished in a creditable eighth place in the First Division. Woodward had been able to play consistently this year, taking part in 27 League matches, though he only scored 4 goals. But his contribution to the team's success was beyond question and it had been another fine year for him. It was also to be his last full year in top-class football.

At the end of the season, he led England's amateurs on another tour, this time to Scandinavia, losing to Denmark 3-0 and beating Sweden 5-1 and 5-0, Woodward contributing one and two goals respectively. These were to be the last matches he played before the First World War.

With the declaration of war against Germany in August, Woodward volunteered his services to King and Country (see chapter four). However, football went on and Chelsea continued to take part in both the First Division and the FA Cup. While still stationed in England, Woodward was able to get leave on occasion to play. His first match was against Sheffield United on 8 March 1915 when he helped his team to a 1-1 draw at Bramall Lane.

Following Chelsea's success in reaching the FA Cup final after beating Aston Villa 2-0 in the semi-final, they applied for leave for their star international so that he could play in the big event. The cup final was due to be played on 24 April. Woodward obtained the necessary leave and to get back in to match fitness he played at centre forward in the two preceding League matches at Stamford Bridge: against West Bromwich Albion, when he scored a goal in Chelsea's 4-1 victory and against Manchester United, when he again scored, though this time it was the Pensioners' only goal in their 3-1 defeat. In spite of hardly playing top-class football all season, he showed that he had lost none of his skill.

On the morning of the cup final itself, Lieutenant Woodward travelled with the Chelsea team to Old Trafford for the match. Until the morning of the match, it was not clear whether Bob Thomson, who was Chelsea's regular centre forward that season and had played in the previous cup rounds, would be fit enough to play as he was recovering from an injury. When he finally declared himself fit the Chelsea management were faced with something of a dilemma. But they were saved from having to make a decision, when Woodward declared that he had no wish to play if it would deny Thomson his place in the side. He said that if all three inside forwards were fit he had no wish to deprive them of the prized final medal which they all fully deserved. And so he sacrificed the coveted honour of leading his team into the FA Cup final as he thought this would be unfair to those who had played all season. Instead, Woodward watched from the stands as his team lost 3-0 to Sheffield United.

FIRST AUSTRIA-HUNGARY TOUR (1908)

At the invitation of Austria-Hungary, the England football team took on a four-match tour of that country at the end of the 1908 season. Two matches were to be played against Austria, one against Hungary and one against Bohemia, which, although given full international status, was, in effect, a province of the Hapsburg Empire.

The tour carried much more significance than a mere football tour, as Europe had divided up into two major power blocs, the Triple Alliance (formed in 1882 between Germany, Austria-Hungary and Italy) and the new Triple Entente (formed only the year before in 1907, between Great Britain, France and Russia). With the forming of the Triple Entente, the Triple Alliance felt threatened and diplomacy between the countries involved was very delicate at this period, with great efforts being put into avoiding conflict while at the same time not wishing to give the appearance of being weak.

It was in the middle of this tension therefore that a national team from one of the Triple Entente countries, Great Britain, went off to tour one of the Triple Alliance countries, Austria-Hungary. Given the delicacy of the situation and the need for the utmost diplomacy, there was no better man the English could chose to captain their team than Vivian Woodward. And so, in early June 1908, Woodward and his team arrived in Vienna ready for their first match against the Austrian national side.

The first match was played on 6 June. The weather conditions were very poor, as only hours before the match was due to start a tremendous thunderstorm had broken over the ground completely flooding it. With just two or three hours to go before kick-off it seemed the match would have to be abandoned, but a band of locals got to work and gradually improved the pitch enough for the game to start. However, they weren't able to completely clear the pitch of water and for the first half hour there was a considerable stretch of turf on the English left wing which was actually underwater. The playing surface on this side was treacherous and it was almost impossible to maintain a foothold. Both the English and the Austrian teams were at full strength.

As well as the poor conditions, the English were also handicapped by the fact that the ground was narrower than they were used to and – what with this and the fact that the left wing was a no-go area for at least the first thirty minutes of the match – their area of operation was very much restricted with the forwards in particular not finding sufficient room to manoeuvre. In addition to which, the conditions made it easier for the Austrians to pack their goalmouth with players to prevent the ball going into the net. So, although Austria were very much on the defensive right from the start, it was 21 minutes before England managed to score their first goal, a fine shot from the inside left, James Windridge. Seventeen minutes later, he added a second and, almost immediately from the kick-off, Woodward, playing at inside right, added a third, leaving the score at half-time at 3-0 to the visitors.

Austria managed to score 11 minutes after the kick-off, but with the pitch now drying out and England getting used to the narrow confines of the playing area, they took control of the game and penned the Austrians in their own half for the rest of the game. Centre forward George Hilsdon added two more goals and George Bridgett, the outside left, a sixth – making the final score 6-1 to England.

Two days later, Woodward once again led his team against the Austrians, this time on a different pitch, which was a full 70 yards wide, and under much better weather conditions. For the Austrian players the match seemed a matter of do-or-die as they played much more energetically than in the first match, tackling fiercely and trying to break out of their own half. In spite of this improved performance and enthusiasm, however, they were once again unable to cope with the sustained brilliance of their opponents. The forward line in particular was at its very best, Woodward in particular was said to be in dazzling form, while Windridge was 'as sinuous as an eel'. It was generally agreed by all present that this was the best exhibition of football ever seen in Vienna, which was fortunate as amongst those present at the game were the representatives of FIFA, who were meeting in conference in the city at the time and were particularly vociferous in their expressions of admiration for the English game. As a consequence, the game itself became very one-sided, with the final score being 11-1 to England. The entire forward line finished up on the score sheet with Woodward, playing at inside right, scoring four of the goals. Francis Bradshaw, who had replaced Hilsdon at centre forward contributed a hat-trick, with one each coming from Bridgett, Windridge and John Rutherford, as well as the right half, Benjamin Warren.

At the end of the match, the winners were accorded a flattering ovation and left their scene of triumph to the accompaniment of cheering from all parts of the ground. The following day the English team embarked on a boat journey along the Danube, arriving fourteen hours later in the twin cities of Buda and Pest. They were immediately whisked off to a reception and, on the following morning, for a sightseeing tour of the city.

That afternoon, 10 June, the team took on the Hungarian national side. They were given a magnificent reception as they entered the field, in particular the captain, Vivian Woodward, who was wearing a Hungarian scarf he had been presented with earlier. When the crowd saw this the cheering was doubled, the compliment to them being much appreciated.

The weather was fine, but the ground was very hard and the players found it difficult to control the ball to begin with, but they soon settled down and, once again, the English forwards put on a magnificent exhibition of football with Woodward in his most brilliant form. The first goal for England came after 11 minutes when Woodward pounced and, following one of his renowned solo runs, placed the ball in the back of the net beyond the goalkeeper's reach. By half-time the score had reached 4-0.

Almost immediately from the kick-off, Rutherford set off on an electric touchline run and crossed a perfect ball right to the feet of Hilsdon, who had no difficulty in finding the goal. Two more goals followed and the final score was England 7 Hungary 0. It should, in fact, have been 8-0, as Bridgett smashed the ball so hard between the posts that it hit the stay at the back of the net and bounced out onto the field of play. The referee, who was some distance away, did not see what happened and disallowed England's claim for a goal. Once again, the England team was enthusiastically cheered off the field.

The last of the four tour matches was against Bohemia, played on 13 June. The game was due to begin in the afternoon, but it was so hot that the kick-off was postponed to 6.00 p.m. Even so, the heat was terrific as play commenced and the English players found the conditions very trying. Once again, the ground was very hard and the ball bounced around unpredictably – which, to some extent, brought the England team down to the Bohemians' level. As a consequence, England, in the shape of Hilsdon, only managed to score one goal in the first half.

For once, everything was not going England's way, but five minutes after the start of the second half, a penalty was awarded against Bohemia and Hilsdon scored his second from the spot. This penalty had two effects. Firstly, on the field of play, it settled the English down, who, with a two-goal cushion, shook off their nerves and began to play a bit better, eventually adding two more goals to finally take the game 4-0. The second was off the field, where the locals were incensed by the penalty. As it happened, the referee for this match was an Englishman, Mr Lewis, and it was felt that his decision to award the penalty was a biased one and completely unjustified. The crowd got very excited and agitated and, after the match, some of the spectators attacked and badly beat Mr Lewis.

Nevertheless, the England team were still entertained to dinner in the evening by the Bohemian Football Association, much to the relief, no doubt, of the British Foreign Office, who could well have done without the incident at such a delicate time.

SECOND AUSTRIA-HUNGARY TOUR (1909)

Following the success of the 1908 Austria-Hungary tour, the English team were invited back again the following year, this time to play three internationals, against Hungary (twice) and Austria. In view of the events of the previous year, it was felt advisable to leave Bohemia off the itinerary this time.

Once again, a full strength England squad, under the captaincy of Vivian Woodward, was chosen and the series of matches started on 29 May 1909 in Buda-Pest, when they took on Hungary. England faced a strong breeze in the first half but they went on to the attack immediately and, after just 4 minutes, Bridgett headed in the first goal. For the rest of the first half the ball remained mostly in the Hungarian half of the field, but the home team defended stubbornly and it wasn't until 10 minutes before half-time that Woodward scored a clever goal, which was added to by Fleming. With the score at 3-0, it looked as though it was going to be another easy victory for England, but just on the stroke of half-time, Hungary's outside left, Jozsef Grosz, managed to pull one back and the teams went in with the score 3-1 to England.

The second half repeated the pattern of the first, with the ball in the Hungarian half for practically the whole time, but a superb goalkeeping display by Laszlo Domonkos prevented

England from running up a big total. In fact, it was Grosz who scored the next goal in the 72nd minute from a breakaway as he lobbed the ball over the English goalkeeper's head, to make the score 3-2. More tremendous pressure by the England forwards followed and, 7 minutes later, a solo run by Woodward culminated in a shot which was deflected into the Hungarian goal, making the final score 4-2 to England.

This goal, in fact, has caused some controversy over the years as to whether it should be credited to Woodward (which it has been) or as an own goal. The significance of this is that if it counts as Woodward's goal then he holds the record for the highest international goals per game ratio: 29 in 23 games. If it is given as an own goal, then his total of 28 in 23 games is equalled by one of his own contemporaries, Steve Bloomer. Accounts of the game are not detailed enough to be able to come to a definitive conclusion, but reports such as they are do seem to suggest it was a shot from Woodward which hit a defender and went in, which would normally today count as a goal for the player who took the shot. In any event, all the record books now credit Woodward with 29 goals and therefore the highest scoring rate.

The result of the match against Hungary was much closer than many had anticipated and great credit was given to the home side by the many spectators for their skilful, plucky and unremitting efforts to get on terms with their powerful opponents. After the match, Woodward commended the Hungarian side and said, 'It is pleasant to be able to place on record that the Hungarians have made immense strides during the last twelve months and I have no hesitation in stating that our opponents today were collectively the strongest side England have ever met on the Continent.'

Much, no doubt, to the Foreign Office's delight, the match was played in a wonderfully sporting spirit and there was not one foul in the whole game.

A record crowd for a football match in Hungary, estimated at 15,000, turned out to watch the second international, played at the Millennium ground in Buda-Pest. The popularity of the visitors ensured they enjoyed a huge reception as they filed onto the field, led by Vivian Woodward. It was said at the time that such was his fame that his name was as well known in Europe as it was in Great Britain.

In contrast to the first encounter, it was Hungary who dashed off at the start in whirlwind fashion, taking the ball deep into the England half. The experience and steadiness of the English defence were enough to hold off the attack, however, and within a short time the ball was back up the other end with the forwards now getting into their stride, completely outwitting and outfoxing their Hungarian opponents. After just 3 minutes, Fleming scored the first goal for England. There then followed an exhibition of football that was as delightful to watch as it was effective in its results. With the whole of the English forward line on the top of its form, there was plenty for the spectators to marvel at and enthuse over. For the Hungarian supporters it was a spellbinding display, the like of which they had never witnessed before and they were generous with their appreciation and applause at the classical movements of the visitors. It was Woodward himself who put in the second goal after 12 minutes and this was followed by a third from Holley 5 minutes later. Woodward grabbed the fourth and, just before half-time, Fleming scored a fifth.

During the half-time interval, all the players were marshalled in front of a special enclosure, where the city's burgomaster and numerous other notabilities were accommodated. Addressing the English players, the burgomaster expressed the thanks of Buda-Pest to the English Football Association and the team itself for having honoured the city with their visit and he voiced his admiration for the wonderful ability shown by the team who had given the Hungarians lessons they would take to heart. In the name of the city he then presented to each of the English players a handsome medal in a case in recognition of the great debt of gratitude they had placed the city under and as a memento of their visit. Amid scenes of remarkable enthusiasm, he presented each of the players with their medal, cordially shaking each one by the hand.

When the second half commenced, the English team seemed to ease off a little. Having established such a big lead they did not put so much energy into their play. The Hungarians, taking advantage of the situation, were able to pull a goal back amid wild cheering from their supporters. The goal seemed to snap England back into life and, shortly afterwards, Woodward added two more goals. Hungary still did not give up and managed to get one more before Holley put in the eighth and last for England.

The final score of 8-2 was a fair reflection of the difference between the two teams. Woodward himself was responsible for four of the goals and many English observers said they had never seen Woodward play a finer game. Of course, the strength of the opposition has to be taken into account but, nevertheless, there can be no doubt that scoring four goals in a full international match was one of the many highlights of his career.

After the match thousands lined the streets from the ground to the hotel where the English players were staying and they were continually cheered as they walked the two miles or so back. It was an extraordinary tribute to the popularity of the English in Hungary and, of course, in those troubled times, held a much deeper significance than just acknowledging the clever skill of the football team.

It is also interesting to note the burgomaster's comments that 'the English team had given the Hungarians lessons they would take to heart', particularly in light of future developments, as they became the first continental team to beat England when, in 1934 in Buda-Pest, they defeated England 2-1 and then later, in 1953, became the first continental team to beat England in England when they won 6-3 at Wembley. They may have taken their time to get there, but perhaps the first seeds of that success were sown by Vivian Woodward and the English touring team of 1909. Fortunately (or unfortunately as it may be!) Woodward lived just long enough to see this outcome of his visit and the lessons he taught the Hungarians.

A large and enthusiastic crowd turned out in Vienna on 1 June to see England play the final game of their tour against Austria. Following the display put on in Buda-Pest, the play in the first half was a little disappointing and the English team did not reach the same heights of skill and ability. It was, however, Woodward who opened the scoring with a goal in the 25th minute – a shot from close quarters, which gave the goalkeeper no chance. Only one more goal was scored before half-time, by Harold Halse, who had replaced Fleming at centre forward for the match.

The second half was quite different as the England team adopted more open methods and decided to use their wings more. In just 3 minutes, Woodward had added a second to his total and a third to England's. Austria then scored from a penalty, but Holley restored England's three-goal lead and then added a fifth. A header from Woodward made it 6-1 while two more from Warren and Halse made the final score Austria 1 England 8.

Once again the English were cheered from the field. On their last night in Austria-Hungary, the players were entertained to a banquet at the Hotel de France by the Austrian Football Association.

Thankfully there were no incidents to mar the visit this time, as there had been in 1908, and the whole exercise was counted a key diplomatic as well as football success.

For Woodward the two tours of 1908 and 1909 were major personal triumphs. He had led his team well through the diplomatic minefield, a particularly nice touch being the wearing of the Hungarian scarf before the match in Buda-Pest on 10 June 1908. On the field itself, in 7 internationals, he had scored 13 goals which included 2 4-goal tallies, one against Austria and one against Hungary, although, as usual, it wasn't just his scoring ability that had won the admiration of the spectators. Once more it was both his ability to combine his forwards and to get them thinking as one and his pinpoint accuracy in passing, which set up attack after attack and laid on goal after goal for his colleagues. His influence on the rest of the team was inspirational and he was able to raise the whole side to new heights.

His play on the pitch and his bearing off it won him thousands of fans in the Austria-Hungary Empire and he was now idolised wherever football was played in Europe. There may indeed be much truth in the opinion at the time that he was now, somewhat like David Beckham a century later, the best known and most famous Englishman on the continent.

SOUTH AFRICA (1910)

The country of South Africa was founded in 1910 from the separate autonomous provinces, such as the Transvaal and the Free State, that had formed part of the British Empire in that region. As part of the celebrations that greeted the founding of the new country, the South Africans invited over from England a national rugby team and a National Association football team. As far as the soccer team was concerned, the South African Football Association asked for a representative side to play a series of matches against local sides as well as three internationals against the full South African side. They specifically asked that the team be a strong one, as, although the South Africans were not up to British standards, they wanted to play against the best as they felt this was the only way they would improve. Consequently, England sent a team of nineteen top-class Football League players, including seven full internationals such as Bristol City's William Wedlock (capped 11 times), Manchester United's George Wall (5) and Swindon's Harold Fleming (4), under the captaincy of Vivian Woodward.

The tour began at the end of May after the English season had finished and continued until the end of July. It was an exhausting schedule, as not only were the English team playing two or three games a week throughout that period and expected to take part in social functions, but they also had vast distances to travel as they went from province to province.

Woodward did not play in the opening match, which saw England beat a Western Province Colonial team 7-1, but took his place at inside right for the second match against

Western Province. He wasted very little time in opening his account in South Africa as, right from the kick-off, the English forwards took the ball into their opponents' penalty area, where Wall passed to Woodward and the latter headed the ball past the South African goalkeeper. Although he scored no more goals in the game, Woodward was instrumental in orchestrating the forward line to score twelve more: the final score being Western Province 0 England 13.

He missed the next couple of games owing to a boil on his leg, but he returned on 8 June in the match against the Free State. Once again he headed the first goal, though this time the match was not such a rout, England running out 4-0 winners.

He was back in action on 11 June against Johannesburg. The South Africans could not believe the standard of play as it became clear that the English could do almost as they pleased. One moment the ball would be in the centre of the field, the next Woodward or Wedlock – his counterpart at inside left – would swing it out to the wing. There was no hesitation, no steadying themselves for an accurate kick; the passes were delivered while the players were travelling at top speed and yet invariably reached their intended targets. The local football supporters considered the accuracy of the passes 'simply marvellous', with the two inside forwards making short or long passes as the occasion demanded. The Johannesburg team and its supporters just could not believe what they were seeing. England ran out 6-1 winners. After the match, Woodward and his team were the guests of the South African Football Association for a show at the Johannesburg Empire.

Just two days later, the English were again in action for a match against West Rand at Krugersdorp. Unfortunately, the pitch was not conducive to skilful football as it was rock hard and was just like playing on concrete. For the first half the English team seemed to potter about like cats on hot bricks. They just could not get a proper hold on the ball and their passing and placing was very little better than that of their inexperienced opponents. The score at the end of the first half was 0-0. In the second half, however, the English team managed to get to grips with the pitch a bit more and finished up putting three past the West Rand goal-keeper, Robertson. The third goal came after Woodward had bamboozled him with a feint and then passed neatly to Fleming, who scored with a low shot.

The following day the English were on their travels again, this time taking the train to Pretoria, where they were met at the station by the mayor and whisked straight off to a reception. The next day they were in action again against a local Pretoria team, winning 4-1; Woodward once again played at inside right. In the evening the team were entertained to dinner at the Grand Hotel and afterwards attended an amateur performance of *Niebe* at the Opera House.

For the first time on the tour, the next match proved to be a close affair as their opponents, the Transvaal, extended them fully and England only just managed to scrape home 1-0. Woodward was once again at inside right. The following game, however, saw England reassert their authority as they took on and beat a Klip River District team, 13-3.

On to Maritzburg on 21 June, the English team arrived by the afternoon mail train to be welcomed by a large crowd at the station. Woodward was rested for the match against the home town team. Nevertheless, his team ran out 6-0 winners.

Three days later, Woodward was back captaining the side against Natal. Once again the English play proved to be a revelation to the local supporters and, by half-time, they were already 5-1 up, Woodward scoring two of the goals. The visitors eased up a little in the second half, with the result that they only added one more goal, the final score being 6-2.

The next match was the first international ever played between England and South Africa. This took place in Durban on 29 June with Woodward taking his place at inside right. The full South African team did not fare any better than the local sides the English had met. The first half was very one-sided and the fact that England did not score a hatful of goals was down mainly to the South African goalkeeper, E. Martin, who played a tremendous game. The Springboks rallied a little in the second half, but the beautiful football played by Woodward and his colleagues once again showed up the deficiencies of the South African game. The final score was 3-0 to England.

Off on their travels again, this time by mail boat, the *Balmoral Castle*, the team arrived at Kingwilliamstown on 30 June after receiving a good send-off from Durban. For the next match against Frontier, Woodward swapped positions and moved to centre forward. He seemed to take a little time to adjust to his new role and was not as prominent in the first half as normal. However he made up for it in the second half, banging in two goals and leading his team to a 7-0 victory.

By this point in the tour, the England team's record was: played 14, won 14, goals for 82, goals against 10. The *Rand Daily Mail* thought this was 'Not too bad', while the *East Rand Express* considered the English team to be "Ot stuff!'

Two days later, England once again took on Frontier. Woodward won the toss and elected to play with the sun at his team's back. Within one minute, England had taken their first shot at goal, J.E. Raine just missing. But the visitors did not have long to wait as, shortly afterwards, Raine once again got the ball, this time on the wing, and centred to Woodward, who headed in, giving the Frontier goalkeeper, Black, no chance. By half-time the score stood at 2-0 to England. In the second half, England, inspired by their captain, were all over the Frontier team, running out eventual 6-0 winners, Woodward adding yet another header to his tally.

After this match, England left Kingwilliamstown for Port Elizabeth, arriving on 5 July. On 6 July, they were back in the field against a Port Elizabeth & District team. Woodward reverted to inside right and once again won the toss, electing to play with the sun at his back. The match was yet another object lesson to the South Africans, finishing up 8-0 to the English, Woodward contributing two. The local paper expressed its opinion that, 'The game, like its predecessors during the tour, was one of skill and science versus imperfect knowledge and lack of combination... Woodward played a clean and sterling game.'

England were to have an even bigger victory three days later when they took on and beat Eastern Province 10-0. Strangely, in the first half they looked a little tentative and only led at half-time 2-0. Woodward, playing in an unaccustomed role at inside left, had scored the first after one of his famous solo runs down the field. In the second half, however, the complexion of the game changed completely with the Eastern Province team being hopelessly outclassed as Woodward took a grip on the game. Shots rained in on the South Africans' goal, with the captain in particular giving an exhibition of heading that frequently drew bursts of applause.

The next match proved to be another one-sided affair as Grahamstown were thrashed 9-0. Following this match the team returned to Johannesburg. At a reception held in their honour, Vivian Woodward, as captain, expressed the gratitude of the whole team for the way they had been treated so far on their visit and he added that the team had enjoyed an excellent journey up from Grahamstown. The following day, with the team finding themselves having a rare rest day (when they were not either playing or travelling), they had a bit of a busman's holiday by watching a match between Krugersdorp Wanderers and Durban Deep.

It was back to serious action, however, on 20 July when a large crowd of over 5,000 people turned out to see the pick of the East Rand Association take on the touring team. In spite of previous results there was a lot of confidence in Vogelfontein, where the match took place, that the East Rand team could compete effectively with the English team. Local partisans pointed out that their boys were famous for their hustling tactics and had been known to succeed where Johannesburg teams had failed in the past.

Unfortunately for them their confidence was misplaced. Within 2 minutes of the start, England had gone 1-0 up. It was a mesmerising move which left the South Africans stunned. Richards got the ball on the halfway line, passed it to Fleming who sent it on to Woodward (back at centre forward for this game). In a neat one–two, he passed it back to Fleming who kicked it forward to Holley who banged it into the net. One minute later, England were 2-0 up, again following some fine work by Fleming and Woodward, this

time with the latter making the final touch. Five minutes
later and another goal. Yet again it was thanks to the work
of Fleming and Woodward, who carved through the East
Rand defence to set up Holley for his second goal. Just
8 minutes gone and the score was already 3-0. The *Rand
Daily Mail* reported that 'The Englishmen were even more
brilliant than usual, and the East Rand defence was absolutely nonplussed'. Following this goal-fest, the next goal
took its time, coming 30 minutes later via a header by
Woodward. A minute later and Woodward had completed
his first hat-trick of the tour, aided once again by Fleming.
The half-time score was 5-0. It seemed like a double-figure
score was a certainty, but, amazingly, no more goals were
scored in the second half. This was partly due to the fact
that the England left-back, Hayes, was injured and had to
go off. Holley took his place, leaving just four forwards up
front. It was possibly Woodward's best performance of the
tour so far. His old genius, both as an individual and as a
team player and organiser of the forward line, was back.
He was also aided by a stunning performance by Harold
Fleming at inside right.

Following this dazzling showing it was straight on to the
second international match against the full South African
side. Woodward remained at centre forward for the game,
which was witnessed by over 15,000 spectators. The form of
the previous game carried over into this one as the attack-
ers quickly got the measure of the South African defence.
The manner in which they combined under Woodward's
leadership was an inspiring spectacle, which delighted the
spectators but conspired to take the heart out of the South
Africans. The final score was 6-2 to the visitors – with the
great man scoring two himself.

As this was England's last appearance in the Rand before going on to finish up their tour in Cape Province, the *Rand Daily Mail* summed up what this first visit of a full England international team under the leadership of the greatest footballer of his era had meant to the Rand and South Africa, and it is worth reprinting in full:

'We have seen the last of the English Football Association team – they went away yesterday morning from Park by the Cape train – and, we have, during the last couple of months, seen the last of the best representatives in any branch of sport that has ever yet come over from England to South Africa.

We have been led to the conclusion that we are not quite the last word in association football. We know something about cricket and rugger, and in good time we hope to be able to put in a soccer team which will give England a good game. That is looking far ahead, but it will come.

"The material is there" says Mr Woodward. One scarcely wants a higher opinion and, even though it came "after dinner", one knows that this gentleman was honest as well as kind.

The departure of the English team yesterday was a sort of triumphal procession along the reef. There were numerous enthusiasts on Park Station in the morning, and everyone tried to shake hands with, and wish a good journey to, our illustrious visitors.

Taking it all round there never has been such a successful tour. The English Association has reason to be very proud of the bearing of the men on the field and off. The "professional" has never before made such a good impression in South Africa, and the English amateur from the soccer ranks has never been so welcome as during the tour.'

For the next match against Western Province, Woodward reverted to inside left. Once again it was a one-sided match, with Woodward commanding the forward line in such a way that it worked like a well-oiled machine. A splendid opportunist, he seemed to know instinctively exactly the right player to pass to and was able to execute the necessary pass with perfect precision. He also managed to score two goals himself in the 9-0 rout.

The third international was the next and final match of the tour. And, just for once, it was a hard-fought contest, with South Africa actually leading 2-1 at half-time. Once again however, the South African players had more than met their match in Vivian Woodward. In spite of being behind, he marshalled his team admirably and was involved in every one of the touring team's goals, including scoring two himself, as England eventually ran out 6-3 victors.

After the match, the South African Football Association entertained the English team to a banquet at the Mount Nelson Hotel. In his speech, the South African FA President said that 'at the end of the tour perhaps better than at any time, they knew how the English FA had responded to their request that an absolutely representative team should be sent. The team had a splendid record. Both on and off the field there had been no single incident to mar the visit.' He added that 'great keenness had been shown right through the tour by the visiting team and that no doubt the great abilities of their captain had done much to bring about the team's great success'.

In proposing a toast to the South African team, Vivian Woodward said that he had just concluded the best tour he had ever had or hoped to have, and he believed no association was better managed. He believed that South

Africa was going to be a very big force in soccer football in the future, and that was because they had behind them a very fine association. He heartily congratulated England's opponents of today and predicted that the next team that came would have a very warm time. He thanked his own team for supporting him in every possible way, and said that South Africa was a great sporting country. In conclusion, he presented a silver cigarette case to Mr Ferdinand Hughes, the England manager, who had accompanied the team throughout the tour. And so the team returned to face the rigours of the next English season – all except Woodward himself, who decided to stay on for a short holiday.

There is no doubt the tour was a triumph for both England and Woodward. The team itself had played 23 matches and won them all, scoring 138 goals to 16. As for Vivian Woodward, after a slightly hesitant start, he had returned to his very best form, completely outclassing the South Africans. His leadership and play were of the very highest order. He could command and combine his forwards like no other player of his time; he could pass and distribute the ball with unerring accuracy and, when the chance arose, he could put the ball into the back of the net with the best of them. And, as always, he never once resorted to questionable tactics. Off the field he had been an exemplary ambassador for England. He was courteous and kind to his hosts and never said a word out of place at the many functions to which he was invited and at which, as captain, he was called upon to speak.

England could not have found a better to man to lead them.

A cartoon published in the 30 June 1910 edition of the *Rand Daily Mail* summing up the differing fortunes of the two English touring teams then currently in South Africa. On the same day as the soccer team beat South Africa in the first international, the rugby team was beaten by Griqua.

LONDON OLYMPIC GAMES (1908)

With the 1908 Olympic Games being held in London it was only natural that, because of Great Britain's pre-eminence in the sport, association football should at last be officially recognised by the International Olympic Committee (IOC) as a fully fledged Olympic sport – thereby becoming the first team sport to be so recognised. Although not officially part of the Games, football had been played as an exhibition sport at all three previous modern Olympics: 1896, 1900 and 1904. After a small exhibition in Athens in

1896, a bigger tournament was held at the 1900 Olympic Games in Paris, but each country competing was represented by club sides rather than by full international teams. The unofficial gold medal was won by Great Britain, represented by Upton Park FC. In the 1904 United States of America Olympics held in St Louis, a very small exhibition tournament took place consisting of just three club sides, St Rose and Christian Brother College, both of St Louis, and Galt Football Club from Canada. The tournament was won by Galt FC and, although no gold medal was awarded at the Games, the IOC subsequently awarded an unofficial one to Canada.

Under the rules of the time, only amateurs were eligible for the Olympic Games, so it was natural therefore that the Great Britain selectors should turn to the greatest amateur of them all, Vivian Woodward, to captain the side – which included all the top English amateurs of the time as representatives of Great Britain as a whole. So much so that it was felt by many that the result of the competition was a foregone conclusion and that all Great Britain had to do was turn up to be awarded the gold medal, so far in front of the rest of the world were the British.

Originally eight teams had entered the 1908 competition in London, but after Hungary and Bohemia both withdrew owing to political trouble in their own countries, the six left taking part were Great Britain, France 'A', France 'B', Sweden, Denmark and Holland. The tournament opened on 19 October with a match between Denmark and France B, which Denmark won 9-0.

The next day Great Britain entered the fray against Sweden. Vivian Woodward took his place in the team at inside right. Right from the start it could be seen that the British forwards were completely outclassing the Swedish team and when Woodward and A. Berry (the outside right) began to interchange places, the back and half-back opposed to them were completely bewildered. Although the Swedes had the first shot at goal, it was soon apparent that they were in for a drubbing. Four goals came in quick succession for the British team, the second being scored by Woodward. Although, after this early onslaught, the Swedish team rallied a little, three more goals finished up in the back of their net before half-time, the third of those being scored by Woodward.

For almost half an hour after the interval the Swedes managed to hold their own and even managed to score through their inside right, G. Bergstroem, but this only served to wake Great Britain up again and before the end of the match five more goals had gone in, making the final score Great Britain 12 Sweden 1.

In the first semi-final, Denmark demolished the French A team 17-1 and, although Great Britain were still the tournament favourites, this score line did much to suggest the gold medal was not the certainty it had originally appeared.

Holland were Great Britain's opponents in the other semi-final. Once again, Woodward was at inside right. From the start it was obvious that Holland would not be the pushovers that Sweden were. They were strong and fast, quick on the ball and clever with their feet. The forwards were skilled at passing but their shooting was not all it could be. Also, they seemed to be lacking somewhat in confidence and may have been overawed by having to face players of the calibre of Woodward. However, they played well and it was not until minutes before half-time that Great Britain managed to break through their defence and score the first goal, though even this was a lucky strike as the centre forward,

H. Stapley, backheeled the ball somewhat speculatively, only to see it trickle into the net off the Dutch goalkeeper's hand and the post. Great Britain took more control in the second half as they scored three more to make the final score 4-0. Woodward did not score, but, as usual, had rallied his troops well after an initially doubtful start.

And so the scene was set for the first official Olympic Games football final with Great Britain, captained by Vivian Woodward again playing at inside right, taking on Denmark. Right from the start it was obvious that Denmark were going to try and mark Woodward out of the game. He had obviously been pinpointed as the danger man and, for a time, the plan worked as Woodward was unable to get a grip on the play. Great Britain's first goal was somewhat lucky as the Danish goalkeeper, L. Drescher, slipped just as F. Chapman took a shot. After that the Danish half-back line continually blocked the British attacks and were looking every bit as good as the home team.

Their excellent play continued after half-time, when they started with a vigorous rush and for some time definitely had the best of the game, though they were let down a little by their forwards whose shooting left something to be desired. The British team were looking for something special from their captain to inspire them and, true to form, they got it. After 20 minutes of the second half, at last he managed to elude his markers and score with a magnificent shot that inspired his team to greater things. However, Denmark also seemed to raise their game and the last 25 minutes of the match saw some wonderful football as both teams played at their very best. The game went from end to end but, in the end, no more goals were scored and Great Britain finished as 2-0 victors.

On 24 October 1908, a very proud Vivian Woodward received the first officially recognised Olympic football gold medal from the Rt-Hon. J. Bell, the Lord Mayor of London.

STOCKHOLM OLYMPIC GAMES (1912)

In the run-up to the 1912 Olympic Games, there was much debate on the International Olympic Committee about what criteria should be used for deciding which games should be included in future Olympics. It was felt that only games or sports which had worldwide appeal should be included and that games particular to one country or region should be excluded. This argument affected football, insofar as it was held that football was at its most advanced in Northern and Central Europe and that other parts of the world had a long way to go to match countries such as Great Britain, the Scandinavian countries, Holland and Hungary. Nevertheless there was no denying that football did have worldwide appeal and so it was agreed that it should continue to remain an integral part of the Olympic programme. Strangely, one of those arguing most strongly against the inclusion of football was the Swedish Football Association; strange because the 1912 Olympics were due to be held in Stockholm.

The Olympic Committee agreed that every nation affiliated to the Federation Internationale de Football Association (FIFA) would be eligible to send up to four teams to the Olympics. This was done so that England, Ireland, Scotland and Wales could send separate teams. FIFA itself, however, considered it 'most desirable' that each competing nation should send just one team and this wish was complied with squads of thirty-three players were allowed for each nation, being eleven named first team players plus twenty-two reserves.

The 1912 Olympic Games opened on 5 May. Woodward's place in Great Britain's heart was recognised when he was given the great honour of carrying the British flag at the opening ceremony.

The matches were due to take place between 29 June and 3 July. Altogether, thirteen teams entered: Austria, Belgium, Denmark, Finland, France, Germany, Great Britain, Holland, Hungary, Italy, Norway, Russia and Sweden – thus giving some credence to the original argument of those who had opposed the inclusion of football on the grounds that it was a Northern and Central European game only.

The tournament was played on a strict knockout basis and, with France and Belgium both withdrawing, the first round consisted of just two matches: Finland *v*. Italy and Austria *v*. Germany with the rest, including Great Britain, obtaining byes.

Great Britain's first match came in the second round against Hungary. It took place on Saturday 30 June in front of 7,000 spectators at the Rasunda Stadium in Stockholm. Once again, the Great Britain selectors had entrusted the captaincy to Vivian Woodward, who took his place for the first match at inside right. Hungary began well and for the first 15 minutes much of the play was in Great Britain's half, but the defence stood up well and no goals were conceded – even a penalty was saved by the British goalkeeper, Ivan Sharpe. After this faltering start, Great Britain took command and H. Walden, the centre forward, soon found the back of the Hungarian net twice in quick succession. Just after the second goal an injury put Britain's centre half, E. Hanney, out of the game and the inside left, Gordon Hoare, was moved back to cover the centre of the field, leaving just four forwards up front. As always, Woodward rose to the occasion and he marshalled his forwards magnificently to cover the deficiency; 3 minutes before half-time, the captain himself scored with a beautiful shot from a well-centred corner.

Although only playing with ten men, the second half turned into a rout for Great Britain as they took complete command of the game, thanks to a large extent to Woodward's brilliant tactical play. Four more goals followed, of which Woodward scored one, making the final score 7-0. Great Britain had won the game with confident play in front of goal as well as fine combination and the individual skill of the team.

Great Britain were now through to the semi-final, meeting Finland on Thursday 2 July. Finland were considered such an easy team to beat that a number of players were rested to keep them fresh for the final, which the Great Britain selectors were sure they would reach. Woodward, however, did play at his customary Olympic position of inside right.

Unfortunately for the spectators, the selectors were right, and the game proved to be very one-sided and not at all exciting. Woodward commanded the forward line with his usual brilliance and tactical awareness and within 5 minutes Great Britain were 2-0 up. Ten minutes later a penalty was awarded against Finland, but the British team, including Woodward, considered that the referee had made a bad decision and when the penalty was taken it was ostentatiously kicked over the bar as they had no wish to take advantage of what they saw as a poor ruling. After that, the British team toyed with the Finns and passed the ball around amongst themselves, so the score at the end of the first half remained at 2-0.

The second half continued as the first had finished. There were some delightful examples of combination play between the forwards and half-backs but no power was put into the shots and it was to be 32 minutes before Walden put in the third goal. In the meantime the crowd had begun to chant 'We want more g-o-a-l-s'. Five minutes later, Woodward obliged with his first and the team's fourth of the match. And that was how the scores finished, with Great Britain going through to the final with a 4-0 win.

The final, which took place in front of 25,000 spectators at the Olympic Stadium at 7.00 p.m. on Thursday 4 July, was a repeat of the 1908 final, with Great Britain taking on Denmark. The rested players returned and Great Britain put out its strongest possible team. Denmark kicked off, but it was Great Britain who made the first attack. However it came to nothing and for the first 10 minutes the ball passed up and down the field as neither team took control. At this point, Woodward, having got the measure of the Danes, steadied his forward line and a well-executed attack, which included most of the forwards, ended in a finely taken goal by Walden. After this Great Britain continued to attack with vigour and assurance. Although the British forwards dominated the field, the second goal came about as the result of a mistake by one of the Danes, Harald Hansen, who mistimed a backpass into the path of Britain's inside left, Gordon Hoare, leaving the Danish goalkeeper no chance.

This second goal seemed to fire-up the Danish XI, particularly the half-back line who gradually began to dominate midfield and their first goal came from a splendid pass from their right half, C. Buchwald, to their centre forward, Anton Olsen, who drove in a lightning shot from about twenty-five metres. This goal had the effect of pouring oil on the Danish fire and they managed to step up their game even more and, for once, the Great Britain team seemed to have met their match. Unfortunately for the Danes, however, Buchwald fell and dislocated his elbow and had to be taken off, thus reducing the Danish team to ten men. His place at right half was taken by the inside left, Sophus Nielsen.

This incident ended the Danish chances as the British team now took every opportunity that came their way and within 3 minutes went 4-1 up, both goals being the result of brilliant forward combination play, masterminded by Woodward. This was how the score remained until half-time.

The Danes reorganised their team for the second half and seemed to take on a new lease of life and even managed to pull one back. This goal made the British team uneasy. Woodward raised his colleagues' morale, which had shown signs of sagging and worked hard to keep the ball in the Danish half. A number of shots were sent in by the British forward line, but Denmark were lucky in having such an outstanding goalkeeper in Sophus Hansen, who was able to stop everything thrown at him. With no more goals being scored at either end, the final score was 4-2 to Great Britain, who thus retained their gold medal. With Holland beating Finland 9-0 in the play-off for third place, the gold, silver and bronze medals went to exactly the same teams that had won them in 1908. This is the only time the first three places have been filled by the same three teams in successive Olympic Football tournaments.

Once again, it was a very proud Vivian Woodward who received the gold medal, this time from Gustavus Adolphus, the King of Sweden.

FOUR

THE FIRST WORLD WAR
(1914-1919)

On 8 September 1914, just over a month after Great Britain had declared war on Germany, Vivian Woodward signed up to do his bit in the Territorial Army as No. 889 Private V.J. Woodward of the 5th City of London Rifle Corps. On 1 February 1915 he was promoted to lance corporal. In the meantime, he had applied for a temporary commission in the regular army, 'for the period of the war' – giving as his referees, Mr J.F. Wall, secretary of the Football Association, and his old mentor, Mr A.S. Wilson, headmaster of Ascham College, Clacton-on-Sea. On his application form his measurements were given as height: 5 feet 10½ inches, girth when fully expanded 36¼ inches and range of expansion 37½ inches. His vision was described as 'good' and his physical development, not surprisingly, also as 'good'.

His application was successful and on 9 February 1915, he was transferred to the 17th Service (Football) Battalion of the Middlesex Regiment as second lieutenant. In order to instil camaraderie amongst the officers and men, many battalions were formed from individual localities or trades and professions. The Football Battalion had been founded in London on 12 December 1914 by the Rt-Hon. W. Joynson Hicks MP, and included some of the leading players of the day such as Northampton's Walter Tull (the first black officer to serve in the British Army), and the international player Evelyn Lintott. By the time Woodward signed up some 200 recruits had been enrolled from London with another 400 from the Provinces.

The Football Battalion was initially posted to Salisbury Plain for training but, on 17 November 1915, by which time Woodward had been promoted to temporary captain, an advance guard proceeded on active service to France followed the next day by the rest of the battalion. There seems to be no record of which party Woodward was in, but by 19 November the whole battalion was back together again at Pont de Bricques and then moved on to Thiennes, arriving on 20 November. The battalion diary notes that 'As we had entrained at 4.30 p.m. the previous day and the mode of travelling was in cattle trucks everyone was pleased to alight.' They then marched to billets in Les Ciseaux. The following morning, Woodward and his fellow footballers had their first taste of the war as they could hear the booming of enemy guns in the distance. They were some sixteen miles from the front line.

They stayed in Les Ciseaux for three days before marching on to Isbergues and then Guarbecque. On 9 December they continued to Annequin Fosse, just two miles from the front. On 10 December they were at last sent to where the action was and spent the day digging trenches and filling sandbags. They stayed in the trenches at Annequin until 22 December, when they were given a rest and moved back to Beuvry just in time for the holiday. The battalion diary noted that '25th being Xmas day as far as possible the usual festivities were indulged in'.

A recruiting cartoon for the 17th Service (Football) Battalion of the Middlesex Regiment.

On 10 January 1916, the battalion football team played the 2nd South Staffs, unsurprisingly beating them 6-0. There must have been fierce competition to get into the Football Battalion's football team! No names have been recorded, so it is not known if Woodward actually played in this match.

On 15 January, the battalion returned to the trenches and on 22 January the battalion diary records, 'Front line still. Capt V.J. Woodward wounded'. During a two-week period in the trenches the Football Battalion lost four killed and thirty-three wounded, mostly as a result of rifle grenades.

Woodward's wound was to his leg and was, like most of his fellow wounded colleagues, caused by a hand grenade. It was serious enough for him to return home. On 6 February he left Dieppe for Dover, arriving later the same day. On his return he was examined by an army doctor who found that a portion of hand grenade had lodged in his right thigh, just above the lower limit of his femur. This was removed. On 16 March he went before the Army Medical Board and was found to be unfit for duty for a period of six weeks. On 13 April he appeared again and, although the progress of his leg seemed to be satisfactory, he was given another six weeks' certificate, but it was felt he might be able to carry out light duties in Great Britain earlier.

However, things did not go quite as well as hoped and, on his next appearance before the Board, they found that 'since his last Board he has suffered from a general dermatitis with occasional elevation of temperature attributed by his medical attendant to the effects of his wound. The Board suggest the possibility of scabies. His general health is considerably impaired.' He was given a further six weeks' extension of sick leave.

On 1 July, the Board found that his 'dermatitis is quite well and his general health is much improved. Sleeps and eats well. Up to the present he has not tried much exercise. His wound is firmly healed.' A further one month's leave was granted.

At the next Board on 1 August he was found to be completely recovered and ready for duty and so, on 13 August, he was ordered to return to the British Expeditionary Force and to report to the Folkestone Embarkation Office on 15 August. He rejoined his battalion on 18 August and was straight back into action in the trenches. In a four-day period from 22 August to 26 August, the battalion again lost four killed and eighteen wounded. Fortunately, this time, Woodward was not one of them.

A general holiday for the battalion was declared on 6 September and a sports day held. After this day off, reality returned for Woodward and the Football Battalion as they suffered heavy shelling from the enemy. On 17 September their trenches were destroyed and it began to rain heavily. Working parties continued all day and night, in most unpleasant conditions, to repair the trenches. On 18 September, at about four in the afternoon, the Germans fired a few trench mortars at them. The men took cover including eleven of them who sheltered in the rear entrance to the trench. Just as they did so, a mine blew up where they were, emitting poisonous gas and killing all of them. Altogether, fourteen of the battalion were killed that afternoon together with six wounded, two of whom later died from their wounds. After that horrific afternoon, things quietened down a little and for the next couple of months they witnessed few fatal incidents.

On 5 December 1916, the Brigade Inter-Company Football Tournament commenced. The final was eventually won by the Football Battalion who beat the 2nd South Staffs 2-0. An Inter-Battalion Football Tournament was then organised. This resulted in two victories for the

17th Middlesex over the 1st Kings by 12-0 and by 10-0, over the 2nd South Staffs 6-1 and over the 34th Brigade RFA, in the final, 2-1. Unfortunately it is not known who played in these matches, but it seems more than likely that Captain Woodward would have played a prominent part, even in a battalion full of footballers.

In March 1917, the Football Battalion was on the move again, this time to Biefvillers, but, before they could move on to Oppy Wood, their next theatre of operation, Vivian Woodward had made a decision to apply for a transfer out of the Football Battalion to become a physical training instructor. Consequently he was sent to the Third Army for a trial period, which began on 26 April 1917, and then on to the First Army Infantry School. He was then sent back to England to report to the Physical and Recreation Training School Headquarters at Aldershot to complete his training as a physical training instructor. He eventually finished his course one year later and returned to the First Army in France.

When the end of the war came later in 1918, Captain Woodward remained in France and became coach to the British Army Football team, organising a number of matches. Early in 1919, the team moved to new quarters in Brussels. During this period they played a number of Army 'international' matches in an 'Inter-Theatre-of-War Championship'. One match, against the Belgian Army, was played back in England at Woodward's old stamping ground, Stamford Bridge, in early March. He played at inside left but was handicapped by a centre forward, Johnson, who was too slow and wasted many of Woodward's passes. In a surprise result the Belgian Army managed to win 2-1. After a return match in which the English team performed much better, beating the Belgian Army 4-2, the English

Army met the French Army on 8 May in the final of the Championship back in England, again at Stamford Bridge. The French Army scored the first goal of the match, but it was Woodward himself who put in the equaliser 10 minutes later. Two more goals from the English followed with one from the French, leaving the final score at 3-2 to the English Army. At the conclusion of the game, the Prince of Wales distributed the medals to each team, including one to the English captain, V.J. Woodward.

In fact this was not Woodward's first return to Stamford Bridge since the war ended as he had been called up twice by Chelsea to play in the wartime competition, the London Combination. On 4 January 1919 he had scored one goal in Chelsea's 3-0 victory over local rivals Fulham and, on 21 April, he played, but didn't score, in the 3-0 win over Queen's Park Rangers. This was to be the last occasion on which he turned out for Chelsea as the directors felt he was now becoming too old to take a regular place in the team when proper League football returned the following season.

Woodward was eventually demobilised on 23 May 1919 and returned to his new home at The Towers, Weeley Heath, near Clacton.

FIVE

RETURN TO CLACTON
(1919-1920)

With the war over, a public meeting was held on 9 August 1919 in the Carlton Hotel, Clacton with a view to reviving Clacton Town Football Club, which had been dormant since 1914. The general view was favourable and, on 30 August, the reformed club advertised in the *Clacton Graphic* for players to come and join them. The team entered the revived Essex & Suffolk Border League, along with Colchester Athletic, Culver Street Ironworks, Paxman's Athletic, Severall's Asylum and Parkeston GER amongst others. They also entered the Essex Junior Cup, the Stope's Cup, the Worthington Evans Hospital Cup and the Pearson Cup.

It was reported in the paper that 'Vivian J. Woodward, who has decided to retire from football, has been invited to become a member of the committee of the local club as he is at present living in the district'. Woodward had indeed made a decision to retire from active football after the Inter-Theatre-of-War Championship Final on 8 May, but he was persuaded back on to the pitch 'for one last time' by Chelmsford on 6 December when he played in their Athenian League match against Hampstead Town. Unfortunately, Chelmsford lost the match 4-2.

Having played again, the bug bit and Woodward agreed to help out his first club, Clacton, should they find themselves short of players. It wasn't long before the call came. On 20 December 1919, Woodward returned to the field in a Worthington Evans first round tie away at Culver Street Ironworks in Colchester. It was a late call-up to the team and had it been known that he would be playing there is no doubt that the 600-strong crowd would have been far larger.

Woodward was soon back in the thick of the action. After a few minutes, playing at centre forward, he sent through a pass to Frederick Baxfield, whose shot was just cleared by the Culver Street goalkeeper. Shortly afterwards, the positions were reversed and Baxfield centred to Woodward. Woodward made no mistake and put in a cleverly placed goal. At half-time the score was Culver Street 1 Clacton 3. Unfortunately for Clacton they could not keep up the momentum in the second half and the score finished at 4-4.

For three-quarters of the match the Clacton forwards played together as if they had been united for months. Both the inside forwards, Phillips and Baxfield, were given opportunities that rarely came their way and it was Woodward who was responsible. Although closely marked by the opposing centre half, he made openings for his colleagues and gave glimpses of the clever footwork for which he had become so famous over so many years. Not surprisingly, however, he began to tire towards the end of the game and Culver Street were allowed back into the match. During the game the Culver Street right-back made a number of dubious tackles and was cautioned by the referee. Woodward also had occasion to speak to him, giving him the benefit of his years of experience with some timely advice.

Woodward agreed to assist his old club again in the replay, due to be played on Clacton's Old Road ground on Boxing Day. His decision to turn out spread like wildfire around the town with the result that on the day of the match the attendance was beyond the club's wildest expectations. As the whistle blew for the match to start, there was still a queue, three or four deep, reaching from the pay box back for at least fifty yards. All previous attendance records for the ground were eclipsed.

It was not a happy start for the Seasiders as Culver Street scored in the opening minutes. However, when the game re-started the home team took control and attacked repeatedly. Several shots went wide but at last Clacton's inside left, Frederick Bruce, equalised. The goal was followed by an exhibition of subtle footwork the like of which had not been seen for many a year in Clacton as Woodward began to take control. When he then put his side into the lead with a brilliant low shot, the crowd went wild with cheering. With the inside right, E. Cooper, adding a third soon after, the score at half-time was 3-1 to Clacton.

Soon after the resumption, a combined forward movement ended in Woodward netting his second and Clacton's fourth. The cheering and applause that followed this goal even outdid that for his first goal and must have reminded him of his days at White Hart Lane or Stamford Bridge or on the international stage.

In the end, Clacton ran out easy 7-2 winners. Once again, Woodward had shown his true class with his clever footwork completely foxing his opponents and his accurate passes setting up many opportunities for his two inside men. This time it was noticeable that Woodward lasted the pace much better and he was still as athletic at the end of the match as at the beginning.

Although he turned out again for Clacton's next match against Colchester St Nicholas in the second round of the Worthington Evans Cup and once again played well, he reminded the club that he did not wish to return full time and had only agreed to come back to help out when the team were having difficulty raising enough players.

The next match on 20 January 1920, however, was against Colchester Town at Layer Road in the Pearson Charity Cup. Colchester were playing in a higher league than Clacton and therefore expected to have no difficulty in disposing of them. Clacton felt their only hope of beating them was to persuade Woodward to play. As it happened Clacton did have some difficulty in getting a team together and at the last minute pleaded with Woodward to play again. He finally agreed on the day of the match and the team picked him up at his farm at Weeley Heath. He got into the team's double-decker bus with his hobnailed boots on and covered in mud, having had no time to change.

In spite of Woodward's valiant attempts, the half-time score was Colchester 1 Clacton 0 and as the second half started Colchester were all over Clacton. Talk among the spectators was of a probable 6-0 beating for the Seasiders. Suddenly a complete change came over the game as Clacton retaliated with a vengeance and managed to equalise. Even an injury to Clacton's goal-scorer, Drew, didn't stop them and they continued to press. Woodward looked certain to score at one point but was floored from behind while in the act of shooting and the chance was gone. Heavy rain began to fall as the referee blew for full-time and ordered half an hour's extra time. The rain got heavier and heavier and began to turn to hail. In the middle of all this, Clacton, in the shape of Bruce, netted from a well-placed corner kick and Clacton found themselves in the lead. The teams changed round for the second period of extra-time, but the hail storm got worse and the light was so bad that with just seven minutes to go the referee blew the whistle and abandoned the game. A famous victory was denied Clacton. The local Clacton newspaper, the *Clacton Graphic*, reported ruefully that 'Had the game commenced on time the result of the match would not have been in doubt. The Clacton team were ready, but two or three of the home side had not put in an appearance till 2.40...'

The turnaround after the break was down to Woodward, whose clever play had kept his colleagues always on the go. Once again he appeared to be just as fit in the concluding stages of the game as at the beginning.

Although Woodward now returned to his farming and missed several matches, he agreed to play in the replay of the Pearson Cup match against Colchester Town on 7 February. In yet another magnificent display of football, Clacton scored early on only to see Colchester equalise shortly afterwards. Not long after that, the inside left, Drew, headed into the net just as the Colchester left-back, Youngs, fell prostrate in front of the goal. Although to many it looked suspiciously like a dive, the referee whistled and the goal was not allowed. No further goals came in the first half.

Just after the start of the second half, it was Colchester's turn to go into the lead, but, once again, Woodward led his forwards to a sustained attack on the Colchester goal. Colchester, for their part, decided to pack the defence and try and hold onto their advantage but, just before the final whistle blew, Clacton managed to break through with Drew scoring a last-minute equaliser. As in their first encounter, the two teams faced an extra-time showdown. Early on in this period both Ayton and Drew were injured but carried on and it was, in fact, Ayton who sent in a perfect low centre to Phillips who scored. Spectators' hats, sticks and even overcoats were thrown into the air, accompanied by tumultuous applause which could be heard for miles around. There were no more goals, and so justice was done, as Clacton beat their more illustrious neighbours 3-2. Woodward had once again demonstrated his value as a leader and his deft passes to the wing proved to be the main factor in defeating the Colcestrians. His lightning dashes down the centre continued right until the end of the match. At the age of forty, Woodward was still playing fast and classic football.

Once again, Woodward withdrew from the team after this match, but he was somewhat surprisingly chosen to captain the Essex County team one last time in their match against Suffolk at Layer Road on 4 March. Taking up his position at centre forward he managed to score one stunning goal, but unfortunately could not prevent Suffolk running out 5-4 victors.

Woodward reappeared for Clacton in the Pearson Cup semi-final against Paxman's Athletic. Yet again the match went into extra time and yet again it was Clacton who proved to be the victors. Woodward's fitness was the cause of comment in the *Clacton Graphic*, 'How Vivian maintained the pace all through surprised his supporters, and his deft passes together with his brilliant leadership in no small measure attributed to his side's success.'

His final competitive appearance for Clacton came in the final of the Pearson Cup played on 24 April 1920 against the First Battalion Cheshire Regiment (stationed at Colchester Barracks). About 500 Clacton supporters made the trip to Colchester by charabanc, car, bus and train. Play to begin with was very even and much of it confined to the midfield, but gradually Clacton began to get the upper hand. Ably led by Woodward, the Clacton forwards made ever more frequent visits to the Cheshire's goal area. The first score came after 20 minutes with a goal from Lewis putting Clacton 1-0 up. Shortly afterwards, he scored a second following a neat pass from Woodward. At half-time the score was 2-0 to Clacton.

After the interval, Clacton attacked again and again, Woodward playing a prominent part every time. Twice he practically ran the length of the pitch with one-two passing movements; the first time between himself and Lewis, the second time with Drew. Both times Woodward unselfishly allowed his colleague to have the final touch but both times they missed. Lewis, however, soon made up for his failure to score by netting Clacton's third. There was one final run by Woodward and Lewis, but this time Lewis put the ball over the bar and so the final score remained at Clacton 3 Cheshire Regiment 0.

There was no doubt that the better side had won. And it was Woodward who supplied the ways and means for this to be the case. Just as in the old days, he kept the forward line intact with the unselfish methods that had made his name. Those present at the match felt that Woodward could well have scored himself, but instead preferred to make openings for his colleagues.

The cup was presented to the Clacton captain, Adrian Gilling, by Mr A. Crowther, president of Colchester Town

FC and vice-president of the Essex County Association. After the local photographers had taken their photographs of the team, a *Daily Mirror* photographer appeared and asked if he could take a photograph of Gilling and Woodward holding the cup. This was readily agreed to.

After being entertained to tea, the team made a move back to their charabanc, but were surrounded by an enthusiastic crowd insisting that Gilling hold the trophy up for them to see. On reaching Clacton their approach could be heard from miles away by the cheers and rattles. The team paraded around the town, the streets of which were lined by cheering crowds who apparently 'waved their handkerchiefs and sticks with great gusto'. The team's health was drunk at the Carlton Hotel, headquarters of the Clacton Town Football Club.

For Woodward this was a significant moment. In spite of all the honours he had won, including two Olympic Gold Medals, the one trophy he felt he had missed out on and would never win was the Pearson Cup. He had twice before been in the final on the losing side, and now, at last, at the age of forty, having come out of (an albeit short) retirement he had won it.

On 1 May, the club members, players, officials and supporters met for an evening of 'toast and song' to celebrate their success in their first season of football for five years. In his speech, the club president, Mr Robert Coan, referred to the presence of Vivian Woodward at the celebrations. He said that he thought that he could look back on his football career with more satisfaction than anyone who had ever kicked a ball. He had started with Clacton, had reached the pinnacle of fame, was the ideal of every sport-loving schoolboy throughout the world and had come to 'rest on his oars' with Clacton. He had achieved his success by unselfish and clean play – undoubtedly the rarest ever seen. He urged all the players present to remember the example and 'Play like Vivian'.

At the end of this part of the speech, Vivian Woodward himself stood up to acknowledge Mr Coan's words. His rising was the signal for vociferous cheering and he was visibly moved by the reception afforded him. It was some time before Mr Coan was able to finish his eulogy.

Although the Pearson Cup final the week previously had been Woodward's last competitive match, he had, in fact, played in a friendly earlier that afternoon against Culver Street Iron Works. Culver Street were winners of the Essex Junior Cup, a trophy Clacton had won in the 1899/1900 season. Vivian Woodward was the only survivor of that team still playing. As they had been the opponents that afternoon, the Culver Street team were invited to the celebration evening. In his speech, the Culver Street manager, Mr Tansley, said that his team had always been out to win by endeavouring to follow Vivian Woodward's example.

Vivian Woodward was to play one more friendly match before finally hanging up his boots forever. This took place on 15 September 1920 when he assisted Chelsea against an army team in aid of Earl Haig's ex-officer's fund. Chelsea won 2-0. Perhaps it goes without saying that in this, his final game at the age of forty-one, Vivian Woodward scored both goals.

SIX

RETIREMENT
(1920-1954)

His playing days now definitely over, Woodward retired to his farm at Weeley Heath near Clacton. In spite of his achievements he was never one for the limelight, though he was enticed back into the public eye in 1922 when he refereed a football match held in aid of the London Schools' Hospital Fund at Stamford Bridge in front of the Prince of Wales. The match, between the city school football teams of Birmingham and London, was part of a larger Schools Sports Festival watched by 20,000 to 25,000 spectators and in which over 1,000 children from London schools took part.

As well as retiring from football he had also given up his architectural practice, though he was proud to see that the 1924 Olympic Games were held in Antwerp, in the stadium for which he had designed the main stand. And so, for the most part, he spent the next phase of his life quietly farming and running the dairy business which he had set up in Connaught Avenue, Frinton-on-Sea. For relaxation he spent more time on his hobbies, including photography, fishing and breeding pigeons. Although he was quite content living a peaceful rural life away from the international glamour he had been used to, he nevertheless felt the need to be still involved in football and to put something back in to the game that had been so good to him, and so, when he was asked in 1922 if he would like to become a director of Chelsea, he readily agreed, staying on in that position until 1930.

With the coming of the depression at the end of the 1920s and into the '30s, life proved to be a bit more difficult for him but he battled through without complaining – as was his nature – and when the Second World War broke out, he once again answered his country's call by becoming an ARP warden.

Towards the end of 1949, Woodward became very ill, suffering from nervous exhaustion. He was no longer able to carry on farming or running his business and he was moved into a nursing home in Castlebar Road, Ealing, Middlesex, under the care of a committee set up by the Football Association. As if it wasn't bad enough that he was suffering from nervous exhaustion and stuck in a nursing home, he had a very unfortunate experience in 1950, when Andrew Ralston, a divisional representative of the council of the Football Association, died suddenly at his bedside while visiting him.

Some time after this, in 1953, he was visited by sports journalist and writer, Bruce Harris. He had been told that Woodward was in the nursing home by Mr J.R. Baxter, a former member of the Footballers' Regiment who had served under Captain Woodward and was now a London Transport bus driver. Together the two men went to see Mr Baxter's former commanding officer. The following is Harris's account of the visit:

'We found Woodward bedridden, paralysed, infirm beyond his seventy-four years, well looked after materially. The

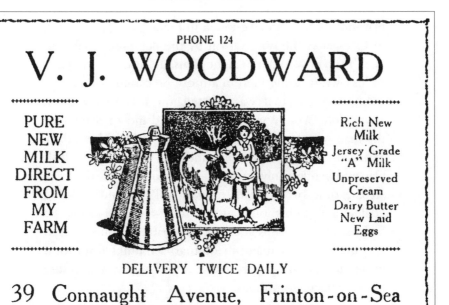

PHONE 124

V. J. WOODWARD

PURE
NEW
MILK
DIRECT
FROM
MY
FARM

Rich New
Milk

Jersey Grade
"A" Milk

Unpreserved
Cream

Dairy Butter
New Laid
Eggs

DELIVERY TWICE DAILY

39 Connaught Avenue, Frinton-on-Sea

This advertisement for Vivian Woodward's dairy business appeared regularly in the East Essex Year Book in the 1920s and '30s.

Football Association and his two former clubs are good to him; relatives visit him often. "But", he told me in halting speech, "no one who used to be with me in football has been to see me for two years. They never come – I wish they would." The FA sent along a television set. It is little use to him, I fear, in his weak health. He gets more from the sound radio at the bedside. He has trouble in reading but can listen now and then. Woodward's heyday as a footballer fell between the century's opening and the 1914-18 war. Then he joined up in the Middlesex Regiment, which according to Mr Baxter had "internationals in every platoon". Woodward, wounded in France, took to farming in Essex after the war, was hit by the depression, failed in health and now, in the twilight of his life lacks the company of his own sporting kind in a room he cannot leave.'

Shortly after that was written, on 1 February 1954, Vivian John Woodward died. It was a sad and lonely end for the man who had once been the toast of English football, admired throughout Europe and a byword for unselfish play and gentlemanly conduct – both on and off the field. At the time of his death he was still England's leading goal-scorer, even though it was forty-five years since he had last played for his country. His death, of course, led to an outpouring of praise in obituary columns from local papers to national papers and it is probably worth noting a few extracts from them.

East Essex Gazette
HE WAS SOCCER'S AMBASSADOR

Regarded as one of the greatest amateur soccer players of all time, Vivian John Woodward, better known locally as 'Jack' and holder of 66 (*sic*) international caps, died on Sunday in an Ealing nursing home. He was seventy-four. Woodward's tally of full and amateur caps – he gained 26 (*sic*) full and 49 (*sic*) amateur – constituted a national record. An old Ascham College boy, he literally finished his illustrious career with the club with which it began – Clacton Town FC, whom he materially assisted to rise from junior to senior status. He quickly made his mark at football, and quite early – in his first game at Ascham College in fact – it was predicted that he would play for England.

A supreme soccer artist, Woodward fascinated crowds with his magnificent ball control. His biggest personal triumph in Essex was when he beat Harwich & Parkeston 'off his own bat', while playing for Chelmsford at Colchester in the Essex Senior Cup. That day he scored three goals, and had a hand in the fourth, Harwich losing 4-1.

Rightly acclaimed as soccer's ambassador, he had a wonderful international career. Abroad he was worshipped, 'Vich ees Woodward?' being a familiar cry.

An amateur through and through, Woodward had only one word for the modern soar in transfer fees. 'Shocking!' was his comment. That was a remark which those who knew him would expect him to make.

Woodward was considered to be the finest centre forward ever to play for England. Which, when it is considered that he succeeded the great G.O. Smith – is remarkable.

Evening News:
VIVIAN WOODWARD, GREAT AMATEUR, DIES AGED 74

Vivian J. Woodward, one of the greatest centre forwards England ever had, died last night, aged seventy-four, at a nursing home at Ealing. He had been ill for four years.

Woodward had a most illustrious career. He was a director of Tottenham Hotspur as well as their centre forward. He was also a director of Chelsea during the time he played for that club.

For many years he was England's centre forward or inside right and, including his amateur and Olympic Games honours, played for England more often than any other player.

He was an out-and-out amateur. Directors of the Spurs and Chelsea have told me they could not get him to charge his bus fares for matches.

He played entirely for his love of the game, and under a code which nowadays would be thought not to belong to this world.

The Times:

Mr Vivian Woodward was to many of my generation the greatest footballer they ever saw, and the living embodiment of the finest spirit of the game. His brilliant play and his outstanding leadership of the victorious British team in the Olympic Games at Stockholm in 1912 will never be forgotten by those who were there; he did much to form the splendid tradition of clean play and sportsmanship which has endured in the Olympic competition ever since.

SEVEN

APPRECIATION

Many words have been written in appreciation of Vivian Woodward's skill as a footballer and conduct as a gentleman. Perhaps two passages in particular, one written 100 years ago at the height of his career, the other, some fifty years later, just after his death, explain the essence of Vivian Woodward and are reproduced below as a summing-up of arguably the greatest centre forward ever to have played for England.

The first is taken from a book called *Association Football and the Men who made it* written by Alfred Gibson and William Pickford, published in 1905:

'Vivian Woodward knows the modern passing game well enough to utilise the best services of his professional comrades, while he is sufficiently individual in style to make the final single-handed dash on goal with a big chance of success. He is not quite heavy enough to "shoulder off" his opponents, but what he lacks in respect of weight he makes up for in sheer skill. The ease and fluency with which he escapes the "attentions" of opposing forwards is hardly less marked than his strong single-handed runs which frequently carries the ball half the length of the field. Woodward is essentially a brainy player. He has no set style. An opponent watching Woodward can never argue that because he has once done a certain thing he will repeat it when the same set of circumstances recur. Because Woodward has acted in a given manner once is a fairly good reason for thinking that he will not repeat himself. The fact is that Woodward has the rare power of thinking on his legs. Many a man with a mind stored full of good things straightaway forgets them all when he rises to address a public meeting. Woodward is like the trained orator. His mind is full of ideas which he is constantly putting into shape, and he has the rarer power of suddenly altering his mind at will. He frequently acts on the inspiration of the moment with splendid results to his side. He can develop a plan as he runs and while the defence is anticipating the conventional pass out to the wing he will swing towards the centre, feint to pass to a comrade, and go sailing on with the ball at his toe. And then heaven help the goalkeeper!

In looking at Woodward he does not impress one as a centre forward who could stand the rough wear and tear of weekly League matches, as his physique is not robust, but he is strong on his legs, and can take an honest "charge" without wincing. A modern centre forward of any class is at once a marked man. Fortunately the football of today, if not less strenuous than that of say twelve years ago, is less open to the charge of unfair play. At any rate, here is Vivian Woodward, week after week, playing with nothing but professionals around him, and after a good many years he has not got a surfeit of the game. It is rather curious that we hardly ever hear a first class amateur complain of rough play. Woodward is certainly not built to be used as a battledore or shuttlecock, but he is quite man enough to look after himself and take his share of the hard knocks that invariably fall more upon the expert than upon the moderate players.

Woodward is easily recognised in a crowd. He is built rather after the greyhound patterns, and moves with great speed and freedom on the field. His is a pleasant face to look upon. To a clear complexion are added a firm mouth, strongly marked eyebrows, and a keen, clear eye that takes in the situation at a glance. One could not mistake him for other than an amateur, and though he has now played many times as centre forward for England, he is not averse to assisting his old original (*sic*) club, Chelmsford, nor does he object to turn out for his beloved county of Essex. It is, of course, as centre forward to Spurs that he is best known. Week in week out, when fit and well, he is found at his post, and when Cup ties call him for midweek matches he is never absent. He is by profession an architect, and besides being a great footballer, he is also an expert cricketer, who can make hundreds in good company. In these days, whilst the game in its most highly developed stages is passing largely into the hands of the paid player, it is well to know that we have still an amateur of the class and calibre of Vivian Woodward, who would scorn to do a mean action, and who is incapable of an unfair one.'

The second comment is from *Spurs: A History of Tottenham Hotspur Football Club* by Julian Holland, published in 1956:

'Less than half a century ago the amateur game was still of such a quality that a slight young man who refused even the price of his bus fares to the ground was 23 times capped for England in the face of all the competition the professionals could provide.

What kind of a player was Vivian Woodward? Woodward was an adept at the "modern" passing game which was gradually replacing the earlier individual style of the Corinthians. But Woodward was also a great dribbler. Lean and fast like a greyhound, he was capable of taking the ball half the length of the field, evading the tackles and the charges of opponents by the deception of his swerving shoulders and the sheer speed of his run. He was not heavy enough to shoulder off opponents challenging for the ball, and in most physical contacts he got the worse of it. Yet it was in such incidents that the greatness of Woodward *as a man* emerged.

Over a decade had gone by since James Oswald, the Notts County centre forward, retired from the game because, as he said, he was tired of being knocked about by unscrupulous defenders, more interested in playing him than the ball. But still the rough play persisted, and in the early years of the century Woodward was a target for a lot of it. But he took it without a murmur. At times, the treatment meted out to him so incensed his professional colleagues that they would begin to retaliate on his behalf. But he was quick to stop them. Bob Steel, who played alongside Woodward in many matches, told me whenever he or another Spurs' player went to "do" an opponent who had been roughing Woodward, the centre forward would soon tell them to stop it. "We're playing this game cleanly," Woodward would say. "There's no need for that kind of nonsense."

Woodward was a natural – a born player of limitless resources. He could think with his legs, altering his mind without pause to exploit a changed situation. If an opening suddenly appeared, he was through it in an instant, the intention to put the ball out to the wing – uppermost in his mind a second before – replaced.

At the distance of half a century, the greatness of Woodward can be measured by the respect in which he was held by the rest of his fellows. He was "their Woodward" and their relation on the field was a close one, even in his last year with the club when he was made a director. The friendship continued even after he announced his retirement, then signed for Chelsea. Football at Tottenham over seventy years has been continuously such a fine and perfect thing that it is enough to say of Woodward that in any side picked from players who have worn Tottenham colours, he would be automatic choice for centre forward.'

And what would we say another five decades on and 100 years since he was at the height of his football powers and fame? Of course, it is hard (if not impossible) to compare players of that era to players of today. Just to give three examples between then and now shows the difference. One hundred years ago there was much more emphasis on individual skill, today we have team talks and tactical plans; managers spend hours analysing the opposition and working out the right format and team formation for dealing with it. Then there were five players in attack, today much more emphasis is put on defence – the standard line-up in 1905 was to have just two full-backs. The third big difference must surely be the fitness levels of today's players compared to then, especially when we are talking about an amateur like Woodward who had his business to run during the week. We would assume that a top team of today would thrash a top team of yesteryear. And yet, when we look at some of the elements that made Woodward great, we can see perhaps the start of the modern methods of play.

He was adept at the passing game. Although he could, when occasion demanded, dribble his way up the field in a long solo run, he was always looking to pass to his colleagues and, certainly, if he felt they had a better chance of scoring than he did, he would make sure the ball got to them. Time and again the old reports mention not just his unselfish play in this regard, but also the way he masterminded his forward line and had them playing as a cohesive machine. In that sense he was taking the place of the modern manager in working out the team's tactics and how their individual styles should be brought together for the good of the whole team. This was a relatively new concept in 1905. He also looked for the flaws in the opposition's defence and played on their weaknesses. As far as defensive football goes, although it is never explicitly mentioned that the forwards would fall back to help out in defence, there must be a clear inference that Woodward did this by the number of times it is mentioned that he ran the whole length of the field, or three-quarters of the field, often firing off one-twos with one of his forward colleagues. His fitness too is often remarked on. He was very fast – 'lean and fast as a greyhound' – and it seemed that this speed continued until the final whistle. He was still able to carry out his solo runs right till the end of the game. In all respects therefore maybe Woodward was ahead of his time and it is probably not too much of an exaggeration to say that he was to some extent responsible for the way the modern game has come about.

Maybe it would be too romantic to say that if an all-time England XI were chosen, Woodward would be an automatic choice. He would have to fight his way through the likes of Dixie Dean, Tommy Lawton, Nat Lofthouse,

Bobby Charlton, Gary Lineker and Alan Shearer to name just a few. But it should not be forgotten that, in spite of these star names, he still holds the record for the most goals per international; he still holds the record for the most goals scored while England captain; he is still the only England captain to score two, let alone four, hat-tricks (and it might have been five, if, in his typically unselfish approach to the game, he hadn't allowed Hilsdon to take a penalty against Ireland in 1909 after scoring two goals) and he is still in the top ten (at number eight) of all-time England goal-scorers. His record for most goals stood until after his death, almost fifty years after he stopped playing international football, when both Tom Finney and Nat Lofthouse reached the 30-goal mark in 1958, but Lofthouse's 30 came from 33 games and Finney's from 76: compare that to Woodward's 29 from 23.

And yet, regardless of those records, scoring goals was not, in fact, Woodward's greatest asset. It was almost a by-product. He did not possess a powerful shot and his goals were scored by his ability to place the ball out of the goalkeeper's reach, whether by foot or by head. His real contribution to any team lucky enough to have him playing for them was his tactical skill, his speed and his pin-point accuracy at passing on the run. He could also, when the occasion demanded it, dribble, baffling and bewildering his opponents with his dazzling close ball control and footwork.

Another aspect of the modern game for the leading players in particular which has to be borne in mind is that of 'role model'. Can there be any doubt that this is where Woodward would have excelled? He was a handsome, charismatic figure who inspired devotion and loyalty amongst both his fellow players and the public in general. His unselfish play was a feature of his game that was remarked on from his very first appearance as a schoolboy until his last season almost thirty years later. He was not in it for personal glory. He was not even in it for the money – as an amateur for his entire career he received no pay, he did not claim for time lost at work, he did not even claim travel expenses. The team was everything to him. Added to this was his admirable attitude to those who fouled him. He took some batterings in his time but he did not believe in retaliation; the referee was there to sort that out. And, although he did miss a number of matches through injury following some of these incidents, he also felt that he could cope with the majority of them. He once said that it was his good balance that enabled him to ride being kicked. He was never once in his career cautioned for foul play.

Off the field he was a devoted family man. Although he was never married himself, he used to visit his married brothers and sisters and spend hours playing with their children, teaching them the rudiments of football and cricket in a pleasant way and not as a lesson. He missed games over the Christmas period for both Tottenham and Chelsea because he wanted to be with his family at that time of year.

As a sporting ambassador he could not be bettered. His leadership of the Austria-Hungary tours and the South African tour at sensitive times in their histories was perfect. He knew exactly how to behave and how to flatter the hosts both on and off the field. When he was in America, even though, on this occasion he was not captain of the touring side, it was he who was chosen as a representative to speak to the American President. And although he was at ease speaking with presidents, he was equally at ease with the average football fan on the terraces. He was idolised by large numbers of football fans not just in this country but all over Europe wherever football was played, yet he never let the adulation go to his head. Football never totally took the place of his family or his business or even his loyalty to the Spencer Cricket Club. It goes without saying that football was a very large part of his life, but it was never all his life. Even as a sport it did not totally dominate him. He played cricket, tennis, billiards and went roller-skating as well – and all to a high standard. It seemed that whatever he did he excelled in. In recognition of all this and as confirmation of his place in British sporting – not just football – hearts he was granted the great honour of carrying the British flag at the 1912 Olympic Games.

Perhaps the epitome of the kind of man Woodward was was summed up when he refused to take the place of Bob Thomson in the Chelsea line-up for the 1915 FA Cup final as he thought it would be unfair on Bob, having played in all the previous rounds, to be denied a cup finalist's medal. In all his long career in top-class football, which included being England captain and Olympic gold medallist, Woodward had never played in the FA Cup final – every player's dream – and yet, here he was throwing away what surely had to be his last chance of ever gaining this honour because it would have been unfair on another player. It was a sacrifice made in the true tradition of Vivian Woodward: *Football's Gentleman*.

APPENDIX

VIVIAN WOODWARD'S SENIOR APPEARANCES AND GOALS

Full internationals for England

Date	Opponent	Venue	Position	Goals	Score (England First)
14.2.03	Ireland	Wolverhampton	C-F	2	4-0
2.3.03	Wales	Portsmouth	C-F	1	2-1
4.4.03	Scotland	Sheffield	C-F	1	1-2
12.3.04	Ireland	Belfast	C-F	0	3-1
9.4.04	Scotland	Glasgow	C-F	0	1-0
25.2.05	Ireland	Middlesbrough	C-F	0	1-1
27.3.05	Wales	Liverpool	C-F	2	3-1
1.4.05	Scotland	Crystal Palace	C-F	0	1-0
6.4.07	Scotland	Newcastle	C-F	0	1-1
15.2.08	Ireland	Belfast	I-R★	1	3-1
16.3.08	Wales	Wrexham	I-R★	3	7-1
4.4.08	Scotland	Glasgow	I-R★	0	1-1
6.6.08	Austria	Vienna	I-R★	1	6-1
8.6.08	Austria	Vienna	I-R★	4	11-1
10.6.08	Hungary	Buda-Pest	I-R★	1	7-0
13.6.08	Bohemia	Prague	I-R★	0	4-0
13.2.09	Ireland	Bradford	I-R★	2	4-0
15.3.09	Wales	Nottingham	I-R	0	2-0

29.5.09	Hungary	Buda–Pest	C-F★	2	4-2
31.5.09	Hungary	Buda–Pest	C-F★	4	8-2
1.6.09	Austria	Vienna	C-F★	3	8-1
12.2.10	Ireland	Belfast	C-F★	0	1-1
13.3.11	Wales	Millwall	I-L	2	3-0

In addition, Woodward played in three unofficial internationals as follows:

29.6.10	S. Africa	Durban	I-R★	0	3-0
23.7:10	S. Africa	Johannesburg	C-F★	2	6-2
30.7.10	S. Africa	Cape Town	C-F★	2	6-3

★ = Captain

Amateur Internationals for England

The following are those officially recognised by FIFA.

1.11.06	France	Paris	C-F	4	15-0
15.12.06	Ireland	Dublin	C-F	1	2-1
1.4.07	Holland	The Hague	C-F	1	8-1
7.12.07	Ireland	Tottenham	C-F★	1	6-1
21.12.07	Holland	Darlington	I-R★	3	12-2
22.2.08	Wales	Stockport	I-R★	1	1-0
23.3.08	France	Park Royal	I-R★	3	12-0
18.4.08	Belgium	Brussels	I-R★	3	8-2
20.4.08	Germany	Berlin	I-R★	2	5-1
20.10.08	Sweden	White City (Olympic Games)	I-R★	2	12-1
22.10.08	Holland	White City (Olympic Games)	I-R★	0	4-0
24.10.08	Denmark	White City (Olympic Games)	I-R★	1	2-0
21.11.08	Ireland	Dublin	?★	0	5-1
17.4.09	Belgium	Tottenham	I-R★	2	11-2
20.5.09	Switzerland	Basle	I-R★	4	9-0
22.5.09	France	Paris	I-R★	1	11-0
6.11.09	Sweden	Hull	I-R★	1	7-0
20.11.09	Ireland	Leeds	I-R★	1	4-4
11.12.09	Holland	Chelsea	I-R★	6	9-1
19.2.10	Wales	Huddersfield	C-F★	1	6-0
18.2.11	Wales	Newtown	I-R★	2	5-1
4.3.11	Belgium	Crystal Palace	I-R★	1	4-0

17.4.11	Holland	Amsterdam	I-R★	0	1-0
25.5.11	Switzerland	Berne	C-F★	1	4-1
21.10.11	Denmark	Park Royal	I-R★	0	3-0
18.11.11	Ireland	Huddersfield	I-R★	1	2-0
17.2.12	Wales	Bishop Auckland	C-F★	0	3-0
16.3.12	Holland	Hull	C-F★	1	4-0
8.4.12	Belgium	Brussels	C-F★	0	2-1
30.6.12	Hungary	Stockholm (Olympic Games)	I-R★	1	7-0
2.7.12	Finland	Stockholm (Olympic Games)	I-R★	0	4-0
4.7.12	Denmark	Stockholm (Olympic Games)	I-R★	0	4-2
5.10.12	Ireland	Belfast	I-R★	0	2-3
9.11.12	Belgium	Swindon	I-R★	2	4-0
8.2.13	Wales	Llandudno	I-R★	1	3-1
21.3.13	Germany	Berlin	C-F★	1	3-0
24.3.13	Holland	The Hague	C-F★	1	1-2
8.11.13	Ireland	Belfast	C-F★	0	2-0
15.11.13	Holland	Hull	C-F★	1	2-1
7.2.14	Wales	Plymouth	I-R★	2	9-1
24.2.14	Belgium	Brussels	I-R★	1	8-1
5.6.14	Denmark	Copenhagen	I-R★	0	0-3
10.6.14	Sweden	Stockholm	C-F★	1	5-1
12.6.14	Sweden	Stockholm	C-F★	2	5-0

Although the Olympic Games matches were played in the name of Great Britain they are recorded in FIFA official records as England games as both times the home countries Football Associations agreed that the England team should represent Great Britain.

Total Appearances:

Full Official Internationals:	23	Goals: 29
Full Unofficial Internationals:	3	Goals: 4
Amateur Internationals	44	Goals: 57

Senior Club Appearances:

Tottenham Hotspur – Southern League:	104	Goals: 44
Tottenham Hotspur – Football League:	27	Goals:18

Tottenham Hotspur – FA Cup:	24	Goals: 5
Chelsea – Football League:	106	Goals: 30
Chelsea – FA Cup:	10	Goals: 4

Other local titles published by Tempus

If you are interested in purchasing other books published by Tempus, or in case you have difficulty finding any
Tempus books in your local bookshop, you can also place orders directly through our website
www.tempus-publishing.com

Forever England
A History Of The National Side
MARK SHAOUL & TONY WILLIAMSON

From the days of amateur gentlemen of the 1870s to the present
day, Forever England is an insightful and fascinating account of the
history of the country's national football team. England's finest hour
in 1966 is covered in detail, as are the other highs and lows of 130
years of international competition. The book also covers the careers of
England's all-time greats and is an essential read for everyone who is
interested in the history of the Three Lions. This enthralling narrative
includes England team line-ups for key games, match reports and
every group table involving England from all major tournaments, and
is richly illustrated with over 200 images.

0 7524 2939 6

Tottenham Hotspur Football Club 1882-1952
Images of Sport
ROY BRAZIER

Named after Harry Hotspur Tottenham have always attracted more style-
conscious supporters and are looked upon as being the most traditional
football side in the country. This selection of includes illustrations and
memorabilia from their earliest days to 1952 and pays special attention to
the great characters that have been associated with the club during this
time including Stanley Briggs, John Camerson, Vivian Woodward and Alf
Ramsey. Essential reading for anyone with an interest in the club today.

0 7524 2044 5

Tottenham Hotspur Football Club Since 1953
Images of Sport
ROY BRAZIER

Over the last 50 years London's most famous football club has enjoyed its fair share of highs and lows. Winning the First Division Championship in 1950/51 and 1960/61 and six FA Cup successes, Tottenham have also enjoyed massive successes in Europe during this time. This pictorial history, which includes many rare photographs, also looks at the great names who have worn Tottenham shirts such as Terry Venables, Jimmy Greaves, Paul Gascoigne and Gary Lineker and will appeal to anyone with an interest in Tottenham Hotspur FC.

0 7524 2924 8

Southend United Football Club
100 Greats
DAVE GOODY & PETER MILES

This volume features 100 of the greatest names in the club's long history. Those selected include stalwarts noted for their longevity and record breaking, such as Sandy Anderson, Billy best and Roy Hollis. Goalscoring masters who dominated the club's history are chosen, like Harold Halse, Sammy McCrory and Brett Angell as well as Goalkeeping legends such as Billy Moore and Paul Sansome. Each of the 100 players are profiled with detailed biographical and statistical records.

0 7524 2177 8

Southend United Football Club
Classic Matches
PETER MILES AND DAVID GOODY

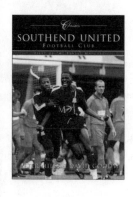

Containing a selection of classic matches from Southend United's near-100-year history, this book will delight all generations of Southend fans. Crushing victories, great comebacks and triumphs over adversity are all vividly recalled from a sideline perspective, as are some of the true greats of the game such as Bert Trautman, Stan Collymore and Gabriel Batstuta. Thoroughly researched and illustrated throughout with contemporary memorabilia.

0-7524-3072-6

Colchester United Football Club 1991/92
A Season to Remember

JEFF WHITEHEAD & MATT HUDSON

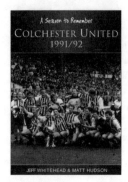

Colchester United faced up to their second season in the GM Vauxhall Conference with major changes in both the boardroom and the manager's hot-seat. On the pitch the new player-manager Roy McDonough faced a gaping hole in the defensive squad after the departure of Ian Atkins and Scott Daniels. The battle for the GM Vauxhall Conference and the prize of a place amongst the Football League elite was about to commence. This match-by match account of that momentous season is an excellent addition to the collection of any Colchester fan.

0 7524 2712 1

The Way U's Were
A Personal History of Colchester United

BERNARD WEBBER

It was a golden age of football. Stan Matthews and Raich Carter were still parading their skills on the big stage and little Colchester United became headline news with one of the most sensational FA Cup runs of all time. Experienced in over 50 years of watching and reporting on Colchester United, Bernard Webber graphically recalls those exciting days and many others, including Colchester's dazzling start to life in the League, in a remarkable piece of soccer memorabilia.

0 7524 3119 6

Clacton-On-Sea
Images of England

NORMAN JACOBS

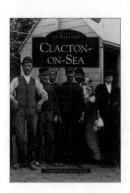

Clacton-on-Sea's motto, *Lux, Salubritas, Felicitas* (Light, Health and Happiness), sums up the main reason for the town's existence. Born in 1871, the brainchild of Victorian entrepreneur Peter Bruff, it was created from nothing to become one of the country's leading seaside resorts. All aspects of the town are recorded in this compelling photographic record: its streets, its shops, its beach, the Pier, its entertainers, the events that shaped it and the people who moulded it.

0 7524 1857 2